Golden Goose

Xu Liu • David Burnett

Golden Goose

The Story of a Peasant Family in Western China

Xu Liu
Sichuan Normal University
Chengdu, Sichuan, China

David Burnett
Sichuan Normal University
Chengdu, Sichuan, China

Reading, UK

ISBN 978-981-13-3773-4   ISBN 978-981-13-3774-1 (eBook)
https://doi.org/10.1007/978-981-13-3774-1

Library of Congress Control Number: 2019934464

© The Editor(s) (if applicable) and The Author(s), under exclusive licence to Springer Nature Singapore Pte Ltd. 2019
This work is subject to copyright. All rights are solely and exclusively licensed by the Publisher, whether the whole or part of the material is concerned, specifically the rights of translation, reprinting, reuse of illustrations, recitation, broadcasting, reproduction on microfilms or in any other physical way, and transmission or information storage and retrieval, electronic adaptation, computer software, or by similar or dissimilar methodology now known or hereafter developed.
The use of general descriptive names, registered names, trademarks, service marks, etc. in this publication does not imply, even in the absence of a specific statement, that such names are exempt from the relevant protective laws and regulations and therefore free for general use.
The publisher, the authors and the editors are safe to assume that the advice and information in this book are believed to be true and accurate at the date of publication. Neither the publisher nor the authors or the editors give a warranty, express or implied, with respect to the material contained herein or for any errors or omissions that may have been made. The publisher remains neutral with regard to jurisdictional claims in published maps and institutional affiliations.

Cover image by the authors

This Palgrave Macmillan imprint is published by the registered company Springer Nature Singapore Pte Ltd.
The registered company address is: 152 Beach Road, #21-01/04 Gateway East, Singapore 189721, Singapore

*This book is dedicated to Zhen
and the indomitable ladies of her generation*

Preface

The dramatic progress in poverty reduction in China over the past three decades is well known. According to the World Bank, more than 500 million people were lifted out of extreme poverty as China's poverty rate fell from 88% in 1981 to 3.1% in 2017 (World Bank 2017). This extraordinary achievement accounts for three-quarters of the reduction in global poverty. It was delivered by a combination of a rapidly expanding labour market, driven by a sustained period of economic growth, and a series of government initiatives mainly affecting rural China.

These 500 million people should not be seen only as a statistic; they are human beings seeking a better life for themselves and their families rather than the life they had previously known—of hunger, sickness, and illiteracy. Our story revolves around Grandma Zhen, born in 1932, a time of war and famine, who in spite of all the difficulties managed to bring up eight children to flourish in modern China. We did not want her story to be written as an objective documentary but rather to provide an account, allowing the members of her family to recount their recollections and opinions. For this reason, most chapters are written in the first person, as if the character is telling their own story. Such narrative telling helps to explain the different accounts given by family members of some of the important events during their lives (Pheonix 2016). We hope the reader will therefore excuse the occasional overlap of content and will appreciate, sometimes with a smile, the different perspectives that emerge.

Nearly all of these accounts were originally told in a distinct dialect of Chinese spoken in the south of Sichuan Province. This was transcribed into Chinese characters and then translated into English. In order to ensure the content was not only accurate but also conveyed the tone the speaker intended, it was later orally translated back into the local dialect and authenticated by the specific family member. In this way, we hope to convey the story of the members of the family as they wish it to be told to an English-speaking audience.

In *Making Stories* (Bruner 2002), Bruner reminds us how much storytelling is a pervasive mode of everyday communication. We hear and tell stories all day long. In everyday storytelling, a well-organized chronology of events is rarely presented. The narratives are selected and evaluated as meaningful for a particular audience, at a particular time. Some stories have been recounted many times over and have been crafted to produce a particular impact. In our study too, events are also rarely connected and arranged in a definite way but come together, sometimes randomly, due to an interruption or request for clarification.

The following chapters are based on a multitude of stories from family members. We have organized them along a timeline of each member's life story, inserting some of the wider historical events occurring in the country, to provide the reader with a sense of continuity and structure. Nevertheless, the authors have tried to keep the stories as close as possible to those related by the narrators. Our aim is to allow the reader to see how the members of the family make sense of their world and their experiences.

Grandma Zhen's story starts in the little village of Jin'e, located in one of the poorest counties in the southwest of China. The village name means "golden goose" and hence the title of this book. The area is known for its extensive region of fertile lowland drained by the Yangtze River and its tributaries, which is surrounded by mountains on all sides. Jin'e is located to the south of the lowland in the foothills that lead across to Yunnan Province in the south and the Tibetan region in the west. Jin'e is typical of the many villages scattered along the valleys between the rolling hills. The villages were joined by rough cart tracks, but even these turned to mud after rain.

In the 1930s, the area was dominated by landowners who rented their fields to the peasants who grew rice, corn, sweet potatoes, and peppers, and raised pigs and chickens. To lease the land, the peasants had to pay the landlords at least 50% of their produce, leaving them sufficient only for their family to live.

The landlords lived in roomy brick-built houses surrounded by stout walls. The walls of the house were painted white, and the window frames were often decorated with flowers and birds. In contrast, the small houses in which the peasants lived were made of wood plastered with mud and usually had a main living room and a couple of bedrooms on either side. A wood-burning stove in the attached kitchen was where food was prepared and cooked.

Throughout the years, the family in this story, like many others, faced the turmoil of the social and economic changes which followed after Mao Zedong and the Chinese Communist Party came to power in 1949. They experienced the hardship of the great famine of 1958–60 and the Cultural Revolution of 1966–76. They had to adjust to a rapidly changing culture that affected all aspects of their lives, including marriage practices, the one-child policy, and expanding education. Through incredible endurance and hard work, the family not only survived but managed to thrive. Theirs is one story out of the millions of the families that have moved from extreme poverty to a comfortable, if not affluent, way of life in modern China.

We particularly want to thank the members of the family for their honesty in sharing their stories. Although the times and events are true, the names have been changed to provide them with some element of privacy. Those with knowledge of Chinese will realize that the names we have given have cultural significance. The four sons are named Chun, Xia, Qiu, Dong (春 夏 秋 冬), meaning "Spring, Summer, Autumn, Winter". The names of the four sisters are Shun, Shi, Hua, Kai (顺 时 花 开). This means "flowers bloom one season after the next," or "everything has its natural order and character."

It is our hope that people from different nations will be able to identify with the members of the family in their struggles and success, tears and laughter. We trust that this account will not only bring mutual understanding between people from different parts of the world but also hope to those who feel they are still struggling on the margins.

Chengdu, China

Xu Liu
David Burnett

REFERENCES

Bruner, J. 2002. *Making Stories: Law, Literature, Life*. New York: Farrar, Straus, and Giroux.

Pheonix, Ann. 2016. "Making Family Stories Political? Telling Varied Narratives of Serial Migration." In *International Handbook on Narrative and Life History*, 356–68.

World Bank. 2017. "Poverty headcount ratio at national poverty lines". https://data.worldbank.org/country/China.

Acknowledgements

This book would not have been possible without the cooperation of Zhen and her family, who kindly shared with us stories of their life experiences and struggles. For David, whose previous experience was of teaching Anthropology in a university and of city life in China, it provided a rare opportunity to enter a world that few foreigners experience. That is, the vast and seldom-visited countryside of China, with its fields, villages, and distinct cultural landscape. For Xu, it has enriched her understanding of how rural people have adapted their everyday lives to the rapid changes of a modernizing society. The countless discussions we have had together and with many people in this area of China have been an invaluable intellectual journey.

We are particularly grateful for the way that Dr Kate Young and Anne Burnett have given their time to edit the text and comment on many issues. They have enabled the writers, more used to writing academic texts, to capture the narratives, and in a better way to communicate the feelings of the people themselves. Other people have also offered critical comments and useful suggestions, and we especially want to thank Dr Alison Lamont. To each of them, we offer our thanks.

Contents

1 Zhen's Story — 1

2 Shun's Story: Number One Daughter — 25

3 Ze's Story: Husband of First Daughter — 43

4 Shi's Story: Second Daughter — 59

5 Hua's Story: Third Daughter — 75

6 Chun's Story: First Son, Fourth Child — 87

7 Xia's Story: Second Son — 99

8 Kai's Story: Fourth Daughter — 113

9 Qiu's Story: Third Son — 127

10 Dong's Story: Fourth Son — 139

11 Grandma Remembers	153
12 Anthropological Themes	163
Glossary	185

Abbreviations

CCP	Communist Party of China, founded 1921
CPPCC	Chinese People's Political Consultative Conference
CPYL	Communist Party Youth League
CVMA	Chinese Veterinary Medical Association
CWF	Countryside Women's Federation
KMT	Kuomintang (also Guomindang/GMD), the Nationalist Party founded 1912
PRC	People's Republic of China, founded in 1949
RMB	The renminbi is the official currency of the PRC and is often called Yuan

Family Tree

xviii FAMILY TREE

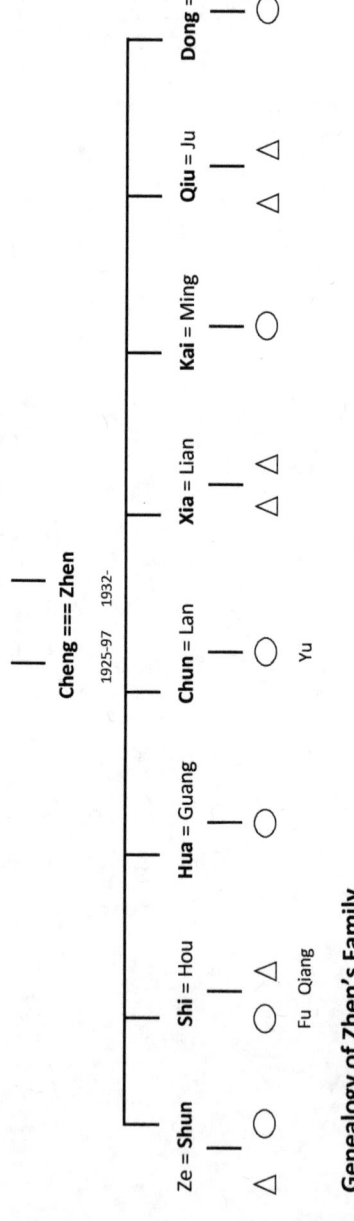

Genealogy of Zhen's Family

Chronology

Year	Family history	General history
1932	Zhen is born	Japanese establish "Manchukuo" under Pu Yi
1934–35		Long march
1936	Cheng arrives in Jin'e	
1942	Cheng apprenticed	
1945		Japanese surrender
1949–50		Civil War in China
1949		People's Republic of China proclaimed
1950		Land reforms begin; new marriage laws introduced; China enters Korean war
1951	Zhen married	Campaign to suppress counter revolutionaries
1952	Literacy campaign	"Four-antis" campaign
1953	Shun (first daughter) is born	First Five-Year Plan; communes introduced
1955	Shi (second daughter) is born	
1957	Hua (third daughter) is born	
1958	Shun at school	"Advanced cooperatives"; struggle against rightists
1959	Baby dies	Famine
1961	Chun (first son) is born	Commune kitchens ended
1963	Shun learns from Lei Fang	Learn from Lei Fang
1966	Shun goes to high school; Ze Red Guard	"Four-olds"; Cultural Revolution starts
1969	Ze sent to the countryside	Ninth Congress of CCP; Purges
1971	Shun goes to college	Lin Bao dies in an aircraft crash
1972	Kai born (fourth daughter)	Nixon visit
1973	Ze manages the commune shop	

Year	Family history	General history
1975	Shun and Ze marry; Shun village teacher; Dong born (fourth son)	
1976		Zhou Enlai dies; Mao dies
1977	Shun's son Jiang is born	
1978		Deng returned to power
1979		One-child policy introduced
1981	Shi marries	
1982		Reform and opening-up introduced
1983	Ze opens shop	
1984	Chun goes to vet college	
1988	Chun marries	
1989	Shi opens shop	
1990	Qiu goes to the city	
1996	Dong graduates and becomes teacher	
1997	Cheng dies	Deng dies; Hong Kong returns to the Motherland;
2001		China joins WTO
2003		Hu Jintao becomes president
2008		World trade recession; Sichuan earthquake
2012		Xi Jinping becomes president
2015		One-child policy ends

CHAPTER 1

Zhen's Story

The year 1931 was a sad year for China. It was the year that Japan invaded the north of our country and established a colony they called Manchuria. In the following year, Japan made Puyi, the last Emperor, the "Chief Executive" of the new state, and then they attacked Shanghai.[1] I was born in that year on the 24th day of the last month of the Chinese calendar (January 1932) in the little village of Jin'e—the name means "golden goose". I know that there is nothing special about Jin'e. It is just one of the hundreds of thousands of villages throughout the countryside of China, but Jin'e is my home.

Jin'e is where my father and grandfather had lived, in the same house in which I have lived for much of my life. Perhaps it is with my father that my story should begin. Die, as I used to call my father, was born in the closing years of the Qin dynasty, which came to an end in 1912. His was a poor peasant family, and to make things worse, Die had a crippled hand. When he reached ten years of age his mother told him he had to leave the house as they couldn't feed him any longer. His parents thought that with his crippled hand he would never be able to make money in the future and would always be a burden to the family. I was always shocked at how my grandma could have done this to her own son, but like most peasants, they were poor and often hungry. Die suddenly found himself homeless and having to make his own way in an uncertain world. Fortunately, some neighbours told him to go to the local landowner as they had heard he wanted a boy to take care of his cows. Die went to see him and was given the job. He lived in the stables with the animals, and although the conditions were hard, he did have somewhere to sleep and some food to eat.

Sometime later, a kind lady saw him and started talking to him. She was sad to hear his story, but was impressed at his endurance and his willingness to work hard. In one of their conversations, she told him that if he ever wanted to start a small stall she would lend him some money. He immediately saw the opportunity and with the money bought a few items to sell in his stall. At this time, soldiers would occasionally come to the area looking for recruits to fight. When they came to Die, he showed them his withered hand, so they could see he would be unable to hold a gun and left him alone.[2]

Through hard work, he began to make some money. In the meanwhile, his parents had slid further into debt and they decided to sell their house and leave the area. Die realized that he now had enough money to buy the house they had vacated. Later, the same lady introduced him to a young woman who came from a family that lived way up in the hills. Her family was wealthier than that of most peasants, and as a child, she had had her feet bound. Tiny feet were considered to be beautiful, and so most daughters of wealthy families had their feet bound. However, she was short and not good looking so she had not been married when younger. Die was pleased to find a woman who would marry him. In time, they had three children: first a boy, then a girl, and finally another boy. I was that girl, and the woman was, of course, my mother whom I called Mu.

Early Years

One of my earliest memories—I was about five years old—is of Mu telling me when she was my age that her feet were tightly bandaged to stop them from growing. Some girls like my mother endured the dreadful pain in the hope that one day they would be able to marry a wealthy man. Mu's feet were so bent that when she stood, she balanced on her heels and toes. I can't remember her ever leaving the house or walking in the street. She missed so many wonderful things. You can imagine how I felt when she suggested I could have Lotus feet too. I refused, but Mu was not angry and did not persist. She said that if the Republican government had rejected the practice,[3] why should she fight with me about binding my feet? Anyway, we were not a rich family with servants to do what we asked. We all needed to work hard to feed ourselves and do the housework.

Looking back over the years, I can see that my parents must have considered me to be a stubborn child wanting my own way. Perhaps that is why I am still alive today even though I am now over 85. I managed to survive the decades whilst many of my friends from my youth have died. I have been able to see my children get good jobs, and my grandchildren do well at school. Some are even studying at universities overseas. Oh, how the world has changed throughout these years!

My father worked hard throughout his life. He managed to rent some land from the local landlord, and through hard work, he harvested a good crop, but he had to give a considerable portion of it to the landlord as rent. This was the life of a peasant at that time! The on-going fighting with Japan meant that there was a shortage of food, so Die had to supplement the food he had grown with some trading. During the slack season for farming, he would take a load of beans and cured tobacco and carry them on his back over the hills to Yunnan Province in the south. The journey over the long narrow trails would sometimes take him a week. There he would sell the beans and tobacco, and buy salt and *danshui*—used for making *tofu*—and carry these back home to sell. He carried as heavy a load as he could so as to make as much money for us as possible. Although my father was proud of his two sons, I knew that he was particularly fond of me, and so I would wait eagerly for his return looking up the path over the hill along which he would come.

Even though my family were only peasants, when my elder brother Qi was old enough he was sent to the little school in our village as was my younger brother. At that time, there were no government schools but only small private schools called *SiShu*, and the classes were held at the home of the teacher. The teacher taught my brothers how to read and write, as well as some of the ancient Chinese classical literature, and the proper ways of behaviour.

Parents would only send their sons unless the family was wealthy when they might also send their daughters or may even have a private tutor for them. There is an old Chinese proverb which says: "Married daughter is like running water." In other words, daughters will eventually leave the family of their birth and become part of another family. I took it to be the normal custom that only boys studied, so I stayed and worked in the house whilst first my elder brother and then my younger brother Hui went to school. Qi was a good student, but Hui tended to be lazy and, to the annoyance of my parents, did not do well at school. I never had the chance to learn to read or write. I could see that a man should learn these things as he would have to work in the fields or even set up a small business. All a girl needed to do was clean the house, cook the food, care for the chickens, and give birth to sons. Every morning I watched my brothers go to school, and I spent the day working in the house until they returned. How I wished I could have gone with them. I thought to myself that when I had children of my own I would send both my sons and my daughters to school so that all my children could learn to read and write, do addition and subtraction.

Die hoped that one day I would marry a high-class young man and become a lady, but we all knew that this was no more than a foolish dream. Even though I wasn't a high-class girl, I wasn't often allowed to go out of the house on my own lest my reputation was spoiled. So, when I had to collect food for the pigs on the hillside, I had to go with a group of other girls. My world was little more than the village and the tree-lined hills around it.

You can therefore imagine my joy when father asked me to go with him to the county town to sell the products he had brought from Yunnan. I was so excited. The day before we went to market, I sorted out my best clothes and carefully cleaned them so I would look nice at the market. We had to leave home early even before it was light so as to get to the market before 8:30 a.m. in the winter and 8:00 a.m. in the summer, otherwise all the best places would be taken. Father would carry two heavy baskets on a pole across his shoulders, and I would carry a smaller load in a basket on my back. He always made me walk in front of him so he could look after me as we travelled. When we got there he knew where the best spots in the market were, and he would quickly set out his things to sell. As he talked to other traders and customers, I would gaze with wonder at all the strange sights. The first few times I went I felt very shy when the town children stared at me, and I would always make sure father was near. Customers would haggle with father, but he was clever and knew how to make a good bargain. I watched how he bargained with different types of people and later he would explain the particular response he had for each of them. At lunchtime, we ate steamed buns that Mu had cooked for us.

We always hoped that trade would be good so that we would not only make a profit but also have less to carry back home. If trade was brisk Die often bought me some sweets, and I always saved some for my brothers. I remember in the winter how the day darkened as we hurried home. Father kept a small torch in his pocket and he would pull this out to light the path as I walked ahead of him. It was always late when we arrived home. I was so tired after the long walk that I would often crawl into bed and fall fast asleep after eating the food Mu had prepared for us. I never complained because I enjoyed those days with Die when he showed me something of the world beyond our village.

Although my parents did not send me to school, they thought that I should learn a trade suitable for a woman, so my mother taught me how to make shoes. In those days, peasants could only afford sandals made from reeds that were skilfully platted and tied. I liked learning new things, so I quickly learned the secret of making good-quality reed shoes. Making them now meant that I could sell them in the market and so contribute a little to the family income.

At that time, one of the most valued skills was that of the potter. You would always know when he was coming into the village because he jingled metal strips to catch people's attention. In those days, most families only had one pot, which was used to cook food for both the family and the pigs. If the pot got broken, it was a disaster, so a person who was able to mend pots was in great demand. Another important skill the villagers valued was that of the veterinarian who would strike a gong to announce his coming. As a child, I never realized that my future life would be so linked to the sound of the gong and the arrival of two strangers in our village.

When I was still a little girl (1936), a woman with a boy of about 11 years of age came to Jin'e from another county in the far north of the province. She was from a wealthy family; her father was a landlord and she had married the son of a landlord. She had two sons by him, but he became sick and after a long illness died. Her situation became desperate. She knew she had to remarry because she had bound feet and couldn't work to take care of her children. As a widow with two children, it was difficult for her to find a husband in her home area, but a matchmaker told her that there was a suitable man in Jin'e. She therefore started the long journey to the south of the Province, travelling by ox cart with her two children. At night, they stayed in simple lodgings along the way. One night she told the waiter at the lodgings of her desperate situation and asked him if he would like to have her two-year-old son. He thought this was a good idea. The next morning, she arose very early leaving her younger child asleep and continued her journey with only her older son.

The man she came to marry in Jin'e was 28 years older than she was. After they married she had no more children, and her husband adopted her son. They changed her son's name to the man's name—Cheng. Because Cheng had grown up in a wealthy family, he was educated. They lived in a house quite near where my family lived. Mu and Cheng's mother spent a lot of time together as with bound feet it was difficult for them to walk far. My elder brother Qi was of a similar age to Cheng, so the boys would play together in their spare time, but being a girl I was not allowed to play with them. Nevertheless, I came to know a lot about Cheng from my brothers.

In 1942, when Cheng was 17 he was apprenticed to Quan, the local veterinarian who lived in the same village as my home. This was in part due to his relationship with Cheng's step-father, but Cheng was also known to be a good conscientious worker. During his apprenticeship, he had to do housework for the vet such as carrying water and coal, and washing clothes. This meant that Cheng went to the vet's house early in the morning and returned home late at night. It was hard work, but he was determined to make the most of the opportunity. Cheng was an apprentice for three years, and then, out of respect for all he had learned from Quan, he continued to work for him for several years. It was the established practice that once an apprentice had completed all his obligations to his master, there would be a formal ceremony to release him from any further obligations. Somehow, this did not happen for Cheng. Then, in 1949, Cheng's step-father died.

As Cheng continued to work for the vet, his position became increasingly difficult because Quan had two sons who had also been taught veterinarian skills. However, the local people recognized that Cheng was the more skilful and preferred him to Quan's sons. The two sons therefore disliked Cheng and often sought to make trouble for him, but Cheng continued to respect his master and members of his family. Since Cheng did not have any relative in the village he was seen as an outsider, and all he could do was to humbly do his work in the hope of building the respect and trust of the villagers.

One day, when I was about 14, a matchmaker came to tell my father about a young man who she said would be a good husband for me. In the countryside, many families liked to marry their daughters when they are young so as to get gifts from the boy's family, which they in turn could use when arranging the marriage of their sons. I still remember the embarrassment I felt when Die told me of the proposal. I was not used to being the centre of any discussion especially with a stranger. I stood still looking at my feet, frightened at what soon might happen. There was little that I could do if father agreed to the proposal. However, I knew father cared for me, and he would do the best for me and the family. So, I waited! After the matchmaker left, father went to the village where the young man's family lived and chatted with some of the local people. He wanted to find out about the family and especially about the character of the young man. He quickly discovered that the family did not have a good reputation and that the son was lazy, so he told the matchmaker that we were not interested in proceeding with the marriage proposal. I was relieved, but realized that more matchmakers would come.

Each time a matchmaker came, Die would find out about the boy's character and his family's wealth and reputation. In the meanwhile, I imagined what it would be like to live in a house I had never seen with people I didn't know and to sleep with a man who was a stranger to me. I knew that I would have no status in that family until I had given birth to a son. Eventually, a matchmaker came representing a man who my father thought could be a good husband for me so he commenced the marriage process. However, when about two-thirds of the way through the negotiations, he heard some bad things about the man and quickly ended them and returned all the gifts from the man's family. My dream was to marry a man who was skilful and could ensure our family had a stable income. I hoped that perhaps he would do business in the town and not just be a peasant farmer.

On 1 October 1949, Chairman Mao formally announced the establishment of the Peoples' Republic of China (PRC) led by the Communist Party of China (CCP). There is a common saying in China: "The Mountains are high and the Emperor is far away." Nevertheless, throughout history changes occurring in China's capital cause waves that spread to every village and transform every family and every person. China was set to enter into a radical new age.

Under Chairman Mao, the government consolidated its popularity among the peasants through land reform, which aimed at allocating the land of rich landowners to poor peasants. Even in Jin'e, some of the richer landowners were beaten, and their fields taken over by the authorities.[4] The Party also sought to raise the status of women, to end foot-binding, child marriage, and opium addiction. I was pleased about these things, but confused when officials closed the temples and told us not to go and worship the Bodhisattva. The temples were part of our lives, and I did not know how we could live without them. When we have difficulties in our life, where could we go to now to ask for help? Nevertheless, we peasants continued to grow the crops, pay our taxes, and live our lives as best we could. Marriages were still arranged, children were born, people died, but changes were happening. I soon realized that as a young woman I had greater freedom than before especially with regard to whom I married. Although Cheng and I didn't have any direct contact, I liked him and I thought that he would make a good husband.

Marriage

By 1950, my elder brother Qi was the manager of the local village cooperative. He and Cheng were good friends and he realized Cheng and I both liked each other. There was however a problem, which led my brother to speak with our father about this. You see, since Cheng's step-father was dead Cheng had no family to help him, so it was difficult for him to make a proposal of marriage. Die didn't approve of the match because Cheng was poor, and Mu said Cheng's mother smoked opium. Then, that year, the Communist Party of China (CCP) introduced a new marriage law which forbade arranged marriages without consent and affirmed the equal rights of both sexes. It attempted both to enhance the status of women and to end child marriage. When Cheng sent a matchmaker to discuss the possibility of our marriage, Die realized that he could not object even though he disapproved.

My parents didn't stop us marrying, but they didn't cooperate with the arrangements either. For one thing, in order to plan a marriage, the man's family needs to know the birthdays of both the man and the woman so as to choose an auspicious date for the wedding. My parents would not give Cheng my birth date and hour,[5] so he had to find this out from friends and neighbours. He was given a confusing variety of dates so he chose one that seemed the best match. Later, I found out that it differed from my true date of birth by ten days. Even today, this makes me smile, and it has become a joke among my grandchildren.

On our wedding day, Cheng invited lots of people to come for the meal. He borrowed tables, chairs, and bowls from the neighbours and about 100 people came, including both my brothers. Some neighbours brought gifts, whereas others cancelled part of the debt Cheng's mother owed them. This meant that Cheng would finally be able to support his own family. Despite all this, my parents still did not approve of our marriage, which made me ashamed at our loss of face. But this was a new age and we didn't have to be constrained by all the traditions of the past. Nonetheless, I was sad because family ties are always important.

After the wedding feast, I went to live as Cheng's wife in his house. The house was like many others in our village with a main door opening into the living room. There was a god-shelf on the wall opposite the door, and two rooms on either side of the living room. Mother-in-law slept in one room, which was also the store, and Cheng and I slept in the other room. As a new bride, when I entered the door I bowed to the family ancestors and was duly introduced to them as custom demanded. They were asked to accept me into the family and to bless our relationship with many sons.

It was only when I moved into Cheng's house that I realized how poor he and his mother actually were. Even though Cheng worked hard as an apprentice, he received little money and his mother wasted a lot of money on her addiction to opium. She had even sold some of their furniture to buy opium. I was so angry when I found out about the situation. I said that from now on I would be in charge of the household income and that mother-in-law must stop buying opium. Cheng had always been respectful to his mother, but he knew that I was right and this was the only way for us to prosper in our married life. Also at this time, the Communist Party demanded that the opium trade be stopped, so I had official support for my position. Later, mother-in-law acknowledged this was a good thing even though it was hard for her to break her addiction.

For a man, marriage is a significant step in life as it means he has become an adult and is taking on the responsibilities for a family. After our marriage, Cheng went to speak to his master to ask him if he could work for himself so that he could earn enough money for his family. His master, the vet, realized that this was necessary for him and gave him a chance to do a major operation on a buffalo. Even though Cheng had done it before, it was always with his master. We both realized how important this was for his future career. On the morning of the operation, I got up early to prepare a good breakfast for him just like I used to do for my father when he left home to go to Yunnan. I prayed that our ancestors would bless him and that the operation would be a success. Cheng told me it was not a difficult challenge for him, but all morning I worried about what was happening, and waited nervously for his return. When he arrived home that evening, I could see from his face that he was happy. He sat down and told me all about the operation and how well it had gone. He would be given 3 kg of rice for his day's work, which meant a lot for us as a new family. That night, I cooked us several eggs to celebrate his success. Cheng and I sat down with his mother. I watched his face shining in the pale yellow light of the kerosene lamp as he talked about his hopes and plans for our life together. I once again encouraged his mother to cease her opium addiction.

In 1951, the same year that we married, land reform was introduced in our area. During this period, a team of actors came to our village to perform political plays about the hardships the landowners caused the peasants. One play I remember was called "White Hair Girl".[6] I still remember that the goal of socialism was said to be "Both up-stairs and down-stairs have light and phone; each day we have a stew of beef and potato to eat."

During this period, landlords and members of their families were abused by the enraged peasants at mass meetings organized by local Communist Party work teams. Their lands and property were divided among the peasants. This was known as the policy of "Sharing of Victory". This caused a lot of excitement because now that we could work for ourselves and not the landowners, we began to think of better ways of increasing productivity. As I was from a peasant family, I was entitled to farm some fields. Cheng, however, was classified as a craftsman, and so he was not entitled to an allocation of land; neither was my mother-in-law because she smoked opium. Nonetheless, after I received my allocation of fields, we worked out how we could cultivate the land better whilst he continued his work as a vet. By the second year, I was able to do this work by myself. We had to pay a portion of the harvest as taxes to the government, but it wasn't too much.

As well as farming the land, I wanted to start a small business. My time helping Die meant that I had learned how to buy and sell in the market, and as we lived not far away from the market, it would have been possible for me to go there to sell our products. When I talked to Cheng about this, he stopped me and said the duty of a farmer is to maintain the land. I was disappointed and did not understand because I thought that I was perfectly able to do both at the same time. In fact, Cheng was worried if we became known as a family that did business, it could result in trouble in the future. Cheng proved to be right! Things were changing in our village. Very soon all religious ceremonies were banned and replaced with political meetings and propaganda sessions. Two of my childhood friends were seriously criticized in public meetings during the Cultural Revolution because they engaged in business which was thought to show traces of capitalist thought. One of my friends committed suicide because she couldn't stand the torment. Whenever I think of this, I am happy that I married a considerate and wise man.

Formerly Cheng had worked for his master, but now as he worked for himself, the farmers wanted him to care for their animals. Cheng got up early in the morning to visit farmers and then came back later in the day to help me with the farm work. We were so happy to have our own land and often discussed how best to cultivate our fields. Most of my time was spent working on the land or at home. That year we were able to reap a really good harvest. We had to give a part of it to the authorities, but still had plenty of food to eat. At the first Spring Festival, after we married (February 1952), Cheng, mother-in-law, and I had a great meal together in which we ate meat. I made new shoes for Cheng and his mother. This was a happy time for us—we both worked hard and looked forward to having our first son.

At one meeting in 1952, the cadres told us that the government had said that literacy was necessary for everyone including us peasants. They encouraged all of us to learn 1000 Chinese characters, to be able to write simple notes, and perform simple calculations using the abacus. As there were few teachers in the countryside, anyone who knew some words became a teacher; we studied how to write the names of animals, vegetables, and farm tools. One peasant taught another, but I think some of the words I learned were not correct. I don't know! Like most of the women my age, my responsibility was to work and look after the family; I had no time for other things. It was hard for me to learn, and I must admit that I have forgotten even the few words I did learn.

Soon the government advocated that throughout the whole country "Mutual Aid Teams" should be established consisting of between 5 and 15 households. Farmers started cooperating with each other by sharing farm tools and animals so as to improve productivity. Another development was that members of the Peasants Association visited each family to ask them to send their children to school. Since there was no school building in our village, the home of the former landowner was taken over as the new school using his chairs. As we did not have a professional teacher, those peasants, like those who had formerly taught my brothers in their own houses, were co-opted as teachers. When we heard that the village would establish a school, Cheng and I were very happy.

Shun Is Born

In September 1953 our first child was born. On that day, Cheng was travelling to some of the outlying villages so I was alone. I had to give birth without any anaesthetic to deal with the pain. Although I was frightened, I knew that I had to be strong for the sake of the baby. I sat on a low seat so I could draw the baby out from between my legs. I had sharpened the shears I used to make shoes and put them in the fire several times then I kept them in cold water so I could use them to cut the umbilical cord. The baby was born early and weighed only 1.5 kg, which probably made the birth easier. I washed her with the water I had heated beforehand, and then lay down to sleep a little before I needed to start cooking our evening meal. When Cheng returned home, he was glad we were safe although with some disappointment that the baby was not a boy. We hoped that next time it would be a boy. We named the little girl Shun.

Our village custom was for the family to invite a fortune-teller to come and predict the baby's fortune; we call this *Suanming*. The fortune-teller uses four numbers that come from the time of birth: the hour, the day, the month, and the year. With these numbers, a fortune-teller is able to tell the person's destiny, their current situation, and the occupation in which they are likely to be most successful. To our surprise and delight, the fortune-teller told us that our little girl was going to support the family just like a son and that we should take great care of her. We didn't know what this would mean, but we remembered these words. Cheng loved this baby very much; when he came back from work, he would always give her a big hug, and even though she was a girl, he would often take her with him when he visited his friends.

The following year I became ill with oedema. I think this came from a small wound on my foot which became infected when I was working in the fields. My whole body became swollen, and I had to go to hospital. As we had no vehicle, four neighbours helped carry me on a stretcher to the hospital which took a whole day. Cheng carried the baby as there was no one to look after her; mother-in-law was left to look after herself. Cheng and I spoke little on the journey. We both knew that when some of our neighbours had gone into hospital they never came out. Cheng and I were fearful that I also would never return home. As we had no other source of income, Cheng had to return home to work and left the child with me in the hospital. After two weeks, I was fully recovered; Cheng paid the bill and the three of us left for home. This was a difficult time as we had no one to help us and there was nothing like medical insurance as there is today.

The Commune

In 1953, government announced what they called "The First-Five Year Plan" (1953–57) that required us to form collective mutual aid groups that were supposed to increase our productivity.[7] The mutual aid groups were later upgraded to become "Elementary Agricultural Cooperatives".[8] Peasants like us could voluntarily join the cooperative by contributing our land and farming tools. In return, the government gave us tools and financial support, while the cooperative managed the land and labour. Usually about 30 households made up a single cooperative. Although we were excited at the idea of progress, we were also worried as we peasants were required to increase food production in order to feed the workers living in the cities. In this period, the food was allocated according to the proportion of land and the amount of work each member did. If a man worked a whole day this was valued at ten points; if a woman worked a whole day she gained eight points. As a man's work was considered harder than that of a woman's, he was allocated the greater amount. However, it was possible for a strong woman to do the heavier work of a man, and so I always chose to do this because it meant I could earn ten points a day and not just eight.

In that year, I gave birth to my second child—a daughter. Once again, I gave birth to her without the help of a midwife. We called the baby Shi. Two years later, I gave birth to a third child—another daughter was born! We named her Hua. Cheng's hope for son was denied him again. Mother-in-law took care of the three girls, whilst I worked in the fields. These were years of hard work and growing hunger. Nevertheless, we remembered the words of the fortune-teller, so when Shun was four years old, we sent her to the kindergarten. Two years later, she went into first grade at the commune primary school. These were difficult times and we could give her only a little food and few clothes. But she was a good girl, and studied well even during winter when the unheated school was bitterly cold.

During these years—I forget which year it was—the communes were instructed to build administration buildings where meetings could be held under the guidance of the local officials. Since Jin'e is located at the centre of a township, the building was built here; in fact, it was built in the field directly across the road from our house. At the sound of the newly installed loudspeaker, Cheng and I would join the other villagers at the meetings to listen to the officials talk about the new policies that were made by the government. As most of us were illiterate, the officials made use of drawings and revolutionary songs. I used to enjoy singing the songs although I struggled to understand some of the things the officials talked about.

In 1958, "Advanced Cooperatives", as they were called, were formed by joining several Elementary Cooperatives together which we were told would further increase our efficiency. Although this was still voluntary, as the Advanced Cooperatives had control of the water supply and we were already committed to a smaller cooperative, what could we do except join the new one? It was at this time, the bonus of land proportion was cancelled[9] and food was allocated only according to the labour a person contributed. To us, it seemed that the fields we had previously been given through the land reform were now being taken away from us. We had to hand over the land to the direction of the officials, and our right to sell the extra we produced was restricted. We were disappointed, but there was nothing we could do. We did not know how this could be done. A system of grain collection was introduced, whereby each district was assigned a quota of agricultural production to give to the State.

All the people in village then became members of the commune, private ownership was entirely abolished, and households were encouraged into state-operated communes. All these new arrangements took place as part of what was called the "Great Leap Forward".[10] The village cadres boasted that if we were bolder, we could make the land yield more. Some said that a *Mou*[11] of land should produce 5000 kg of rice, but we peasants knew this was impossible. No matter how hard we worked, we could manage to produce only 500–600 kg of rice a *Mou*. Even today, with all the modern methods, we can only manage to grow 1000 kg of rice on such a small plot. No wonder we were about to head for disaster.

Then, communal kitchens were introduced. The authorities said that a communal canteen would bring us eight benefits: fixed meal times; the release of more female labourers; provision of cooked meals for bachelors, the disabled, and the old; the collective feeding of livestock; enabling the weak to contribute by working in the canteen; enabling the development of collective activities and family harmony; and the improvement of sanitary conditions. The canteens were designed to feed between 100 and 120 people, and were located near to where there was water and vegetables.

We had never heard of anything like this before. As private cooking was replaced by communal dining, everything we had in our kitchens, such as tables, chairs, cooking utensils and pans had to be given to the communal kitchen. The commune leaders then assigned the uses to which these items were put. Every morning the same officials would assign us jobs for the day. The work was hard and everything we produced had to be given to the commune. We had no food of our own, but depended on the commune for everything. In the early months, people were enthusiastic, but soon many started being lazy and productivity quickly declined. I became increasing concerned for my little daughters, my elderly mother-in-law, and the baby I was then carrying. I always took something with me to do during my rest time such as making shoes.

The canteen provided three meals a day; people came from their jobs and joined the elderly and children to eat. In the first months, people would sit together and chatter loudly. There was enough rice, corn, and fresh vegetables to eat, and some people would even bring home-made pickles. On festivals, the canteen would slaughter a pig to provide meat. Some families however lived far from the canteen, and had to walk a long distance even though it was raining or very hot. Some of the old people and children started complaining that it wasn't easy for them all to come to the canteen and asked if family members could collect the food for them to eat at home. We were fortunate in that we lived quite near the canteen, but even so as mother-in-law did not know how to tell the time, she and the children often missed meals. My elder brother, Qi, worked for the commune and sometimes gave us some of the food he got as part of his salary when he visited us. Cheng also worked for the commune as a vet, and was given 5 kg of rice each month. Although we had only a little food, we were better off than many families.

In the autumn of 1958, we were told that within 15 years our leader Mao Zedong wanted the Chinese economy to surpass that of the United Kingdom and the United States. This was called "Surpassing Britain and Catch up with USA".[12] Steel production was considered as the key to economic growth and so all communes were encouraged to start making iron. The plan was that during the slack farming period each commune should produce iron ore. Although we had never done such a thing before the commune leaders told us to gather stones and cement to make a furnace. Cheng and I were called to go to work at the blast furnace, but I didn't like it at all, as the work was strange and accidents often occurred. We began cutting down trees to provide fuel, and every family was required to bring any metal items they had to be melted down and recast. These included our cooking pots, pans, and bowls. We even went into the hills to look for any iron ore that we could dig up. We did our best, but the metal we made was never very good and we were told that it was of little value. All this work we had done only meant that many of us had been taken away from working the land.

In this year also the Commune leaders began telling us of the start of a new struggle against "Rightists".[13] I had no idea who these people were, but assumed they were former landowners and corrupt officials. We heard that there were many rightists in the cities, who were being denounced by their colleagues. Jin'e was a poor village with few scholars, but I remember the tensions between families increased. Arguments and fights often occurred and people were frightened.

Famine

The weather in 1958 was good and we expected a good harvest, but when it came to autumn much of the crop was not gathered in because so many of us were too busy making iron or working on irrigation projects. We didn't know how much food there was in the communal store, but when winter came, we realized that the grain in the granaries was in short supply. The food served at the commune kitchen became even sparser. We peasants used to call this season "between the green and yellow", because around Spring Festival the fields are bare of both ripe (yellow) and newly sown crops (green). In 1959, there was even less food than usual and everyone knew that a famine was coming.

The village cadres started making regular visits to every family to check if anybody was hiding food in their homes. When they saw smoke coming from your chimney, they immediately came to the door and shouted at us to stop all cooking. Because of their hunger, if people saw a corn cob on the ground they would grab it and eat it raw as they were afraid of being caught and beaten. The cadres told the canteen staff to find ways to increase the amount of food, so the cooks did all sorts of things like adding lots of water to the rice to make it swell. They ground corn stalks and cobs into powder and added it to sweet potato leaves to make something like a cake. Food like this was difficult to swallow, but since this was all we had to eat—we ate it. Then people started getting sick; everyone was frightened for their families.

Many people were so hungry that they stole some of the commune rice. If they were caught, they were publicly beaten especially if they had formerly been landowners. Shun and Shi often worked on commune land, and so it was easy for them to slip sweet potatoes in their pockets. Had they been caught they wouldn't have been beaten because they were children. Shun was able to do this, but Shi was too scared of being caught and beaten that she cried at the very thought of doing it. Sometimes when

Cheng came back from work tired and exhausted, I would find an egg for him to eat. But, the smell of food would draw the children from their beds and they would stand in a line watching him eat by the light of the little lamp. Of course, he would always share the egg with the girls just to see the little smile on their face.

In 1959, my fourth child—another daughter—was born. I told Cheng I thought she might not survive because of the poor food that I had been eating. But, there was another reason I thought that the child would not live—I had had a dream. A week before her birth I dreamt that our family had a dog, but it would not stay at home and continually ran away. Just two days after her birth the baby became ill and died. We buried her at the edge of a field not far from our house. A year later, Cheng was passing by the little grave when he saw a small snake emerge from a hole in the ground. It stopped and looked at him. He spoke quietly to the snake, "I am sorry that it was not your destiny to live with us. You can't live with us now; you must look after yourself." The snake turned and slid back into the hole in the ground.

It was around the Spring Festival that starvation really set in and the weak and the elderly began to die. In the communal care house, many people died of starvation. I hate thinking of that time—the gnawing hunger, the fear for my family, and my own body's continual weakness. These were terrible years. The animals began to die, and when they did, they were quickly butchered and eaten by people. When you are so hungry your eyes are always looking for food be it a grain of rice or a dead bird. Some people filled their stomachs with grass or the bark of trees, or even some types of mud. People hunted for any rat around the house, or any frog in the ponds. The lack of animals and the tiredness of the people brought a strange silence to the village. There were rumours of parents eating their own babies, but I didn't know if that was true or not. No one who has felt such hunger would condemn them!

Cheng was always kind, and asked Shun to take a little food to his old Master. In China, we have an old saying: "He who teaches me for one day is my father for life." Cheng told Shun to wait for him to finish eating otherwise his son would take it from him and eat it all. One day Shun came back to tell us the master wanted to see Cheng; the old vet was starving but grateful for the morsels of food that Cheng had sent him. He told Cheng, "You are a kind man and you will have a good future." Soon afterwards Quan died. In 1960, the condition of the elderly and the sick was very bad. Women and children were becoming physically weak. The adults stopped going to work or even going to the canteen, and went instead to the hills to dig for wild vegetables. The government began giving some food aid, and the new harvest brought us hope.

By 1961, the worst of the famine was over. The land was given back to families to cultivate, the commune canteen was closed, and all the pots and pans were given back to the various families.[14] Each family was given a small plot of land, just 18 metres square. Cheng and I planted corn, wheat, and sweet potato. At the Spring Festival, it had become our family tradition to make rice balls, but the poor conditions in the famine years had made this impossible. So, at the 1961 Spring Festival we used some of our allocation of corn and wheat to exchange with our neighbours for sticky rice. For the first time in four years, we made rice balls to celebrate New Year. The girls were so happy. The following year, a similar exchange wasn't possible so I got some powdered sweet potatoes and used this instead of rice. Although they looked the same as rice balls, the taste was very different. With great excitement, the children looked at the rice balls and quickly reached for them. Shun took one bite and turned to me and asked why they tasted so different from the previous year; Shi however was hungry and quickly ate them. There is a Chinese proverb which says, "One can see how a child's adulthood will be when he is 3 years old, and how his old age will be when he is 7." It means you can see a child's future even in their childhood. I thought at the time that these two girls are so different. I said to Shun, "It is much better than nothing and I hope we can have this every year." Cheng sat quietly, but I could see from his face that he was afraid of the past and unsure of what the future would bring.[15]

A SON

We had three daughters but no son; Cheng felt he was losing face by not having a son to carry on his trade as a vet. Sometimes Cheng would say that it was because of my fate that we did not have sons, so he talked about adopting a boy. I didn't agree with him because I was sure that I would one day give birth to a son, and so we argued. If a wife doesn't bear a son she has little authority in the family, but I continued to state my views because I knew I had done nothing wrong. Cheng persisted in wanting to adopt a boy, and I thought he had in mind his step-father's nephew. I knew the boy, and because he was lazy, I didn't think he would have a good future, so I continued to object. I became pregnant again, and this time Cheng was sure that it must be a son because we believe that if a child dies during delivery or soon after, this changes your fortune. The month before the baby was due Cheng invited a midwife to look after me. I had delivered each of the previous four children myself, but this time Cheng felt that I should definitely have a midwife since he was so convinced the child would be a boy. The midwife was a local woman, older than me, and although she did not have professional education she had a lot of experience helping women give birth. She helped me to relax and encouraged me to scrub my hands and body, and sterilize the instruments. I knew that if there was an emergency she would not be able to help, but she was the best we had in our village.

When a boy was born, there was such joy in our family. Cheng was delighted and said he finally had a successor for both his family name and his skill—we called him Chun. The girls were pleased to have a baby brother, and I was relieved that I had at last given Cheng his much hoped-for son. Cheng arranged a big celebration with 25 tables, enough to seat 200 guests, more than at our wedding those years ago. Again, we borrowed chopsticks and plates from all our neighbours. Traditionally, this sort of celebration was only held by very wealthy people, but Cheng and I were so delighted that we had a son we wanted our friends and family to enjoy a party. The midwife continued to look after our son and me for another 40 days following the birth, and Cheng was happy to pay what for us was a lot of money for her services.

Later, in 1961 Cheng and my brother Qi each bought a piglet. We rebuilt the pigsty, and fed the two piglets on scraps of our food and what we foraged from the hills. Pigs take about a year to grow big and fat, and so by the end of the year, Cheng and Qi slaughtered the two pigs. They gave one to the commune and we kept the other for ourselves. This was the first time that we killed a pig to celebrate the Spring Festival, and the children really enjoyed feasting on the meat. Although we were not wealthy, every Spring Festival since that time we have been able to kill a pig for our celebrations. I would cook the head of the pig in a large pot to which we would keep adding vegetables for each meal throughout Spring Festival. When we had guests for dinner, we would heat the head to make soup. And each day, as there was less and less meat on the head we told the children only to take the vegetables otherwise our guests would get no meat and we would be shamed. The children sometimes saw a little portion of meat, but managed to say "I do not eat meat" or "I've had enough already" and eat the vegetables to fill their stomachs. The famine we had been through had been a terrible time, but we had survived. My daughters

Shun, Shi, and Hua were then aged nine, seven, and five, and my son Chun was over six months.

Then, another problem occurred. There was an increase in tension between Cheng and the sons of his former master due to the competition between them. Cheng worked harder than either of them, so this made them even more jealous as the farmers preferred him to them. Even though Cheng had no relatives in the village, I was born and bred in Jin'e, so we were able to gain the support of the local officials at Cheng's unfair treatment by the sons. Cheng was also good at cooking and the neighbours liked him to be the chef when they were celebrating some occasion. However, his master's two sons were cooks, and sometimes Cheng was asked by a neighbour to cook with the brothers. When this happened, I was always fearful for Cheng's safety, so I would send our two elder daughters with him so that if any difficulty arose the girls could run and tell me. One day, just as I feared, the sons attacked Cheng; they beat him and left him injured. The girls quickly ran to tell me, and I went to the head of the commune who was my uncle. He knew all about the on-going rivalry and managed the incident well. Quan's sons were fined 10 RMB to pay for the medicines needed for Cheng's injuries, which at that time was a lot of money. Then, Cheng's official job as a vet was moved to a nearby town, which avoided any more conflicts.

At one of our commune meetings, I remember an official telling us that Chairman Mao had decreed that it was the poor and lower-middle peasants who would lead the country in the new society. I didn't really know what was meant by this, but it seemed to mean our conditions would get better. Every month poor peasants came to tell stories about the past and what they suffered under the landlords. This was the practice they called "Remember past miseries with the current happiness of today". I could certainly remember past miseries, and hoped that both my girls and boys would have the opportunity of a proper education and a better standard of life. In 1966, some officials came saying that they had come to the countryside to remove any remaining capitalist ideas from among the peasants' thinking, and to teach us quotations of Chairman Mao. Many of us had a copy of the "Little Red Book of Mao Zedong" even though many of us couldn't read.

In 1967, Chairman Mao launched what became known as the "Cultural Revolution".[16] Students were called to leave their colleges and high schools and move to the big cities to destroy the old ways. I heard a radio broadcast which said hundreds of thousands of students were protesting in Beijing, each of them carrying a copy of the Little Red Book. I didn't understand what was happening until some students came to our village and damaged the temple on the hillside. This greatly saddened me, but I said nothing. I was not educated so how could I expect to understand all that was going on. I just wanted to take care of my family, and ensure we had enough to eat.

It used to be the practice in our commune before we started work or before we ate a meal, that everybody would stand and say together, "We wish great Chairman Mao may live ten thousand years, and we wish his close comrade-in-arms the Deputy Commander be healthy and live for ever." The Deputy Commander was Lin Bao.[17] In 1971, we heard that the Deputy Commander had been killed when his aircraft crashed on a flight to the Soviet Union. As we all knew that China had a bad relationship with the Soviet Union at the time, we realized he must have betrayed Chairman Mao. We were all shocked. The next day his name became the object of criticism and his name was no longer included in our wishes.

This same year, another sad thing happened. My sister-in-law, Qi's wife, who was a hard worker and a great help to my brother in bringing up their four children and my elderly parents, contracted a serious illness and died. Her youngest child was only three years old. My brother told me the little boy at dinner time always went to his mother's room and said, "Mummy it's dinner time." He did this every day for half a year until he realized that his mother would never return. At this time, Qi was only 45 and had a good job, so he tried to find a suitable wife. But whenever a woman found out that he had four children and two elderly parents, she did not want to marry him. He finally gave up looking for a wife and tried his best to look after his children and his parents on his own. Whenever we had hard times my older brother would always support me, and apart from Cheng, he was my best friend.

Then, something totally unexpected happened. Our commune had the chance to send a person to study at college who would return to become the official teacher at the commune school. They chose my daughter Shun. I was so proud of her when I heard this, and knew Shun would be very pleased. She was a hard worker, diligent in her studies, and enjoyed learning. As she was from a poor peasant family, the officials said she was the ideal choice, in fact a perfect illustration of Mao's ideal. Shun's fees would not only be paid by the authorities, but she would also receive 3 RMB a month and become a formal worker of the government. I remembered what the old fortune-teller had said after Shun was born. He had been right—Shun could take responsibility like a son.

Notes

1. Puyi (7 February 1906–17 October 1967) was the last Emperor of China and the twelfth and final ruler of the Qing dynasty. On 1 March 1932, he was installed by the Japanese as the Chief Executive of Manchukuo, a puppet state of the Japanese Empire.
2. When the Anti-Japanese war began, the government introduced compulsory military service. All men aged between 18 and 45 were registered for military service. Every year the village head used a lottery to decide who should go to the army. In order to avoid military service, many children of local gentry gave money to beggars or homeless people to take their place.
3. In 1912, the new government of the Republic of China banned the practice of foot-binding although they did not actively implement the law. The practice lingered however in some isolated regions until 1949 when it was outlawed by the Communist government.
4. Long before the Land Reform Law was promulgated on 30 June 1950, the Communist Party had been experimenting with measures to return the land to the peasants. These experiments took various forms wherever the Party had maintained a stronghold, including the Provinces of Jiangxi and Yan'an. Essentially they involved abolishing land ownership by the elite and giving land to the peasants. As a result, many peasant households obtained the deeds for a piece of land for the first time ever. Around 300 million peasants who had little or no land were assigned some 47 million hectares of land plus farm implements, livestock, and buildings.
5. One of the 12 two-hour periods into which the day was traditionally divided, each being given the name of one of the 12 Earthly Branches.
6. The White-Haired Girl (白毛女; Bai Mao Nu) is a Chinese opera by Yan Jinxuan, first performed in 1945 and made into a film in 1950. The opera is about a peasant girl who is persecuted by a landowner and his bullies and flees into the mountains where her hair turns white.
7. The First Five-Year Plan highlighted 694 large and medium-sized industrial projects. To increase agricultural production, Party officials encouraged rural families to cooperate in order to increase their yields. The cooperative process began in 1953, and by 1957, more than 90% of famers were in some form of cooperative arrangement.
8. In autumn 1955, Mao was displeased with the slow pace of economic development, and pushed to increase the production of food and cotton in the countryside.
9. This was the allocation of land formerly owned by the landowners to peasant families, and the areas of land they received depended upon the size of their family.

10. In spring 1958, Mao initiated the "Great Leap Forward" requiring millions of villagers to work for weeks on end on massive building projects.
11. Mou is a Chinese unit of land measurement that varies with location but is commonly 806.65 square yards (0.165 acre, or 666.5 square metres).
12. In the West known as the "Great Leap Forward".
13. The Anti-Rightist Movement (Chinese: 反右运动) lasted from about 1957 to 1959, and consisted of a series of campaigns to purge alleged "rightists" from within the Communist Party (CCP). The definition of rightists varied, sometimes including any critics of the government, but generally, it referred to those intellectuals who appeared to favour capitalism and were against collectivization.
14. After Mao received reports of mass starvation in the countryside, an emergency directive was issued in November 1960 allowing villagers to farm their own plots and engage in side-line occupations. Investigation teams spread over the countryside bringing to light the full dimension of the famine. Large quantities of food were then imported from the West.
15. In January 1962, a gathering of thousands of cadres in Beijing revealed the famine had been man-made, and support for Mao wavered. The famine slowly abated, but continued to claim lives in parts of the countryside until the end of 1962.
16. In 1966, the Cultural Revolution, or more formally the "Great Proletarian Cultural Revolution", was set into motion by Mao Zedong, then Chairman of the Communist Party of China. Its stated aim was to preserve "true" Communist ideology by purging remnants of capitalist and traditional superstition from Chinese society, and to impose Maoist thought as the dominant ideology within the Party.
17. Lin Biao (5 December 1907–13 September 1971) was a Marshal of the People's Republic of China who brought about the Communist victory in the Civil War. Lin died when the plane carrying him and several members of his family crashed in Mongolia on September 13, 1971, allegedly after attempting to assassinate Mao and defect to the Soviet Union.

CHAPTER 2

Shun's Story: Number One Daughter

Ever since I was a child, I knew that Baba and Mu—that is what I called my father and mother—would have liked their first child to have been a boy and that they were disappointed that I was a girl. I was born in 1953, and they named me Shun, which in Chinese means "smoothly" or "favourably". They told me that soon after my birth, they asked a fortune-teller to come and predict my future from the time and date of my birth. My parents were delighted when the fortune-teller told them that I was going to be a special person and that they should take great care of me. I hope that over these past years I have not disappointed them.

When I was five years old, the Communist government introduced one of the greatest changes rural China had ever known in our history. All the traditional family farms were merged into Peoples Communes. I was too young to be aware of this change; all I remember is the commune. I am a child of the commune! I grew up in a world in which peasant farmers shared the land, their tools, and their labour. One of my earliest memories is of the news broadcasts that echoed across the village every morning from the loudspeaker system as people went to work in the fields. Every evening, patriotic music was played to welcome the tired workers home. The commune was the focus of our lives, and as a child, I did not know that this great social experiment was to end up so badly.

Child of the Commune

When I was four years old, I went to kindergarten. Mu told me that as a child, she had always wanted to go to school like her brothers, but her parents didn't agree with her. In those days, peasants only sent their sons to school as girls were seen as being less important to the family. However we were now in a new age, and as the fortune-teller had said that I was a special person, Mu and Baba thought that I should go to school. I think that this was especially important as Mu's second child, Shi (born in 1955), was also a girl, and then in 1957, she gave birth to her third daughter.

After two years in the kindergarten, I went into first grade at the local primary school. School started at around 8 a.m. and finished at around 5 p.m., and every day I would take a bun with me for lunch. The subjects we studied were Chinese, arithmetic, drawing, and singing. I liked school and enjoyed the things we were taught. At that time, the school did not have many facilities so we children had to make our own playthings. Baba made me a skipping rope from the stalks of sweet potatoes and a spinning top from a piece of wood. These were wonderful toys and every day I would take them with me to play with during break time. Sometimes I would exchange them for other children's toys. My memories of playing with the other children are some of the happiest I have of that time, but what I remember most about my early years at school was being hungry and cold.

At home, I had no time to play as, after doing my homework, all my spare time was spent working around the house and looking after my younger sisters, and later my little brother. Grandma Xian, Baba's mother, would look after us as Mu and Baba had to work long hours every day. Grandma and Baba's mother became great friends. Grandma's feet were so small that she found it difficult to keep her balance. I thought that when she walked she looked like a drunken man! Although they both had bound feet, they still wanted to help contribute to the family.

Grandma Xian would help with some of the housework. I remember that we would grind corn together on a big old stone grinder. Grandma Xian would sit next to the grinder and pour corn into the hole at the top, while Shi and I turned the grindstone. Shi and I spent a lot of time with her and I think that is why I always had a deep affection for her. Mu made us work hard and was always strict; she was even strict with Grandma Xian. With so many mouths to feed, food was always limited, so each day Mu would allocate a certain amount of food to each of us. Grandma Xian always got the smallest portion as Mu thought she did not need the energy to work hard, but we knew that Baba would always give her part of his food and also gave some to us girls.

Support for our family also came from "Grandpa Luo" who wasn't really our grandpa, but he did have the same family name as us. He was a bachelor who came to Jin'e in 1950 to work at the agricultural taxation office. As he was then more than 50 years old and unmarried, he had no family in the area; he often came to visit us and we gradually considered him to be part of our family. I remember how he often encouraged me to study hard so that I could get a good job and be able to buy food to eat.

It was at Spring Festival in February 1959 that I first realized something of what was about to come. We were eating dumplings as we always did at this time of year, but somehow they tasted different and not as delicious as I remembered. I asked Mu why they didn't taste so nice, and she merely said that I should be grateful that I had food to eat. I looked across the table at Baba and I saw his eyes were focused on his plate and he looked worried and sad. 1959 and 1960 were hard times for everyone in the village. Children as well as adults suffered. As food became scarcer, we all learned to tighten our belts to stop our stomachs continually growling. As Grandma could not walk far, it was my task to go to the commune kitchen and line up for the daily rations for members of our family at home. The meal was usually no more than a thin soup made from sweet potatoes. I remember one day, as I was returning home from the commune kitchen one of our neighbours called to me and begged me to give her some of our soup. I saw her thin body and dark eyes looking at the container I was carrying. I was frightened and shouted at her "No, no!", and ran home tightly clutching hold of the pot of precious soup. That night I woke with a start, dreaming that someone had stolen my soup. In the darkness I cried!

These were times of hunger especially in the winter when the weather was bitterly cold. I had only two sets of clothes, one for summer and one for winter. I wore them when attending school and they had to last me the whole school year. When clothes became too small for us, they were passed on to a younger brother or sister. I had one coat which I wore nearly all the time during winter. None of us children had sufficient clothes to wear and we shivered in the unheated classroom as we repeated our lessons. I well remember one day when I went to the toilet during the break in class time. The school toilet was a pit latrine located right next to a pigsty. I carefully hung my coat on the partition wall of the pigsty when I went to the toilet. When I had finished and stood up, I saw that my coat was missing. I didn't know where it had gone and my immediate thought was that someone had stolen it, but then I heard the pig grunting and saw that it had dragged my coat into the pigsty and was eating it. There it lay in the mud and filth next to the pig. I quickly reached over the wall and grabbed my coat back, but by now, it was all dirty, torn, and stinking. I was so upset that I just cried. Then, to make things worse, when I got home Mu scolded me saying that I should have been more careful. I remember standing there crying and shouting out that I had been careful. Compared to other families ours was better off because Baba worked for the commune as a vet, which meant he had a stable monthly income. Mu had managed to save a little money, so she was able to buy some cloth to repair my torn coat. I can't tell you how glad I was to have my coat back.

I was always pleased to have the opportunity to study, and I tried to be an excellent student. I learned quickly, but I remember one problem I had. You may think it rather funny, but at the time, I didn't think so. I had difficulty writing the numbers "6" (六, Pinyin: *liu*) and "9" (九, Pinyin: *jiǔ*). The teacher became cross with me for continually getting them wrong; she told me to write the numbers correctly on the blackboard 100 times. I was unhappy because I felt the punishment was unfair; I didn't want to do it! But Baba and Mu said that the teacher was always right and I should accept all of the teacher's requirements. So, slowly in my best writing, I wrote the number nine correctly 100 times on the blackboard. By the time I finished doing this it was late in the evening and the communal meal time was over. I returned home very hungry, but there was no food left in the house. When Mu and Baba got back from work, I told them what had happened. Even though they were tired and hungry themselves, they went out to see what they could find for me to eat. They came back with some sweet potatoes and from it made me some soup. By 1962, the food situation had improved. This was in part due to some of the fields being returned to the families who now worked harder as they knew they would be able to eat more of the actual crops they grew. The collective canteen was eventually closed because the people were then able to cook food at home.

Although I enjoyed doing homework, this was not easy as there was little light in the evenings and we only had one kerosene lamp. Mu would light it, and while she was busy doing housework, my sisters and I would study by the flickering yellow flame. Years later, doctors told me that the strain of reading in such poor light probably weakened my eyes, so that now I struggle to read. The damage done only became obvious when I went to junior high school where I realized I could hardly read the writing on the blackboard.

At that time, schools were also required to pay particular attention to the students' ideological education and moral development. Every Monday morning we would stand in rows in the playground for the flag-raising ceremony and sing the national anthem at the top of our voices. The central themes of our ideological and moral education were "The Five Loves": love of our country, the people, science, work, and the protection of public property. Sometimes the school invited the doctor of the County Hospital to come and tell us how to prevent disease and protect our eyes. A technician from the electricity station also came to tell us how to avoid being struck by lightning and other things. It was not all study—we would have times of fun as well. Every year, for example, we had competitions in writing, calligraphy, painting, singing, rope skipping, shuttlecock spinning, tug of war, and other sports.

On 5 March 1963, an article by Chairman Mao entitled "Learn from Comrade Lei Feng" was published in the national newspapers.[1] Our teacher told us the story of Lei Feng, how he was orphaned when he was only seven years old and that in his teens he joined the army as a soldier. He became well known for his eagerness to work and selflessly serve everyone. We children were encouraged to live like Lei Feng and serve one another. I remember that once when I saw a small pencil laying on the ground my first response was to keep it for myself, but as I knew the teacher would praise me, I gave it to her. She exclaimed that I was a good model just like Lei Feng. I was very pleased!

During the period 1964–66, lessons became more political. Chairman Mao had decreed that poor and lower middle class peasants would lead the country forward in the new society. So each month a representative from a poor peasant family would come to our school to tell us stories of the hard situations they used to face under the landlords. We were taught many of the sayings of Chairman Mao, which I still remember today. An important one for us students was, "Study hard and do better every day" (*Haohao Xuexi, Tiantian Xiangshang*, 好好学习，天天向上). This sentence was posted on the front wall of our classroom and ever since that time schools have continued to do this. To study hard was my goal, and so when I was in the third grade of primary school I became a member of the Young Pioneers.[2] Like my fellow classmates, I considered it a great honour to wear the red scarf of a Young Pioneer. Our teacher told us: "The red scarf is a corner of the flag, and red is the blood of the martyrs. We need to cherish the red scarf in the same way we protect our eyes." Sometimes I wondered whether the red scarf was really made red by blood or not, but I did not ask. Anyway, the red scarf became such a precious symbol that if someone lost their red scarf we considered this a serious offence. The student was required to stand in front of the whole class and to confess their carelessness.

In class, we studied the books of Chairman Mao and pictures of him were posted on the school walls and displayed in the streets. Many people wore Chairman Mao badges to show their allegiance. To be honest, we children had little idea of who he was and we merely copied what we saw the adults doing. Our teacher once asked us if we belonged to the "Left Wing Clique" or "Right Wing Clique".[3] I didn't know what this meant, but I remembered Mu saying that if anybody asked me about political things I should be careful how I answered. So I said, "I am carefree clique." The teacher looked puzzled and asked what I meant. I replied "It is my own clique." The other children laughed, and fortunately, even our teacher smiled!

One thing we children always looked forward to was festivals because this was an occasion we could eat noodles. We started to prepare for the festivals months before by saving a little wheat every day until we had enough to exchange for noodles for the whole family. When the day of the festival arrived, I would run back home from school to get the wheat we had saved to exchange it for noodles at the village mill. My sister Shi and I would rush to finish our homework and any household chores, and get everything ready for our parents return later that night. Then, when all the family had arrived, we would sit down to eat noodles. Nowadays noodles are eaten with many tasty ingredients, but then we ate them only with a little salt; nonetheless, they tasted as if they were the most delicious food I had ever eaten. Once we finished eating the noodles, we would look forward to the next festival.

When I was older, Mu said that I should do some work for the commune. One of my earliest tasks was to fetch water for the commune kitchen so that the cooks could prepare the evening meal of rice. In return, we would get the water that had been used to wash the rice to feed the pigs. This meant I had to carry ten buckets of water from the well to the kitchen. It was hard work but I didn't complain. Sometimes, when I was washing our family's clothes, some cadres whose families did not live in our village would jokingly ask if I would wash their clothes too. Every time this happened, Mu told them to leave their dirty clothes in our house for me to wash. She said it was a little job we could do to help the busy cadres, and so I diligently washed the clothes. Although I did not realize it at the time, our family became well known to the cadres.

In 1966, I passed the enrolment examination for junior high school with a good score, and I started at school in the August. At this time, the college provided only a bed in a dormitory and a supply of hot water at a fixed time every afternoon. The school was 10 kilometres away from home so the first time I went there Baba carried my things on his back all the way—my clothes, bedding, thermal flask, bowl, and pans. The trip took us two and a half hours. As this was the first time I had left the village, I was both excited and afraid. Many of my primary school classmates were unable to continue with their studies because there were only a limited number of places, which were offered in terms of our academic scores. I realized how fortunate I was. It was at this time Chairman Mao was calling on students to fight against the "Four Olds"—Old Customs, Old Culture, Old Habits, and Old Ideas—and continue the great revolution.[4] We heard that many students in Beijing had stopped going to classes and were attending great rallies in Tiananmen Square.

After I had finished my first year in junior high school, revolutionary tours around the country called *Dachuanlian* started.[5] The Party was encouraging all young people to leave school and travel around the country and talk about their revolutionary experiences. I wanted to join in as I thought it sounded exciting, and it would allow me to see life outside. Baba wanted to borrow money from a neighbour to help me, but Mu strongly objected. She was worried that I might get into trouble, and she also thought it wasn't right for a girl of my age to run wild. At the same time, she said there was all kinds of work that the family needed me to do. So, like most of my peers, I had to go back to my village. What I found hardest to bear was that some of our neighbours told their children that even though I had passed the high school entrance examination my studies were wasted. Perhaps this made them feel less embarrassed about the failure of their own children in the examination. Nevertheless, they were right that despite all my hard work I was not able to finish my junior high school. I was regarded by the Party as one of the "educated youth returning to the countryside", which distinguished me from young people from the city who were sent to the countryside who were called "educated youth going to the countryside from the city".

I was then only 14 years old. I continued carrying water for the commune and with my younger sister Shi, who was then about 12, I also carried coal. To collect the coal we had to walk to town once a month with some of the older teenagers from our village. As this involved a three-hour walk each way, we had to leave home early in the morning. Sometimes we didn't have any shoes to wear. Even so, at the beginning we thought it was an exciting adventure because Mu would give us a little money which was enough to buy a bowl of noodles in the town. We arrived at the coal yard around 11:30 am, spent an hour or so collecting coal before preparing to return. The load I had to carry weighed 20 kg, and Shi's load 10 kg.

In the late summer when bamboo shoots were ready, the older teenage girls would steal some of them to take home whilst we younger ones kept watch. Once on our way home as we were walking along the river bank, the heavy load of coal caused me to lose my balance and I slipped down the muddy bank into the river. I heard Shi scream as I plunged into the water. With a bit of a struggle I managed to stand up in the water, but I couldn't climb out of the river. Shi was scared and shouted loudly for someone to come and help me. Fortunately, a nearby adult came and hauled me out of the water. Both Shi and I were scared and upset that I had lost some of our coal.

During one of our trips to the coal yard, we discovered that there was a worker with the same family name as us. His job was transporting coal in an ox cart to various towns in the area. Because we had the same family name, it implied that we had some distant family connection, so I called him "uncle" and we became friends. Every time he saw us carrying a heavy load of coal he felt sorry for us and tried to help us. After he heard that I had slipped into the river and was only saved by a passer-by, he thought that he should do more to help us. He talked with the driver of the ox cart from our village and asked him if it were possible for him to carry some of our coal. As this driver knew our family and our Baba had helped him in the past, he agreed to do this. From that time, Shi and I did not need to go to the town again to get the coal, which was a great relief for both of us.

I still remember in those hardest of days how Grandpa Luo always encouraged Mu and Baba by saying, "Other people are able to live and so can we." Whenever he had the chance to take a child to visit his friends he would take one of us so we could eat some food. I realized that I had to find a way of making more of a contribution to the family income as there were now six children of which I was the eldest. My parents thought that it would be a good idea for me to learn how to make straw mats from a member of Mu's family who was a weaver. I therefore went to stay with her and learned the skill from her. Within four months, I was able to make excellent mats, so I returned home and started teaching my younger sisters the same skills. Baba would go into the countryside to buy the straw from the farmers and brought it back for us to weave. Peasants used straw mats as the base of their beds. They were popular because they were cool in summer and provided some insulation from the cold of winter, but most of all they were cheap. I was responsible for organizing my two younger sisters in making the mats. On the morning of market day, I always got up earlier than they did to check each mat so as to feel confident that all the mats were of an excellent quality. We sold our mats at a very fair price. Sometimes I complained that we sold them so cheaply that we didn't make much profit, but Mu passed on some advice to me from my grandpa. He used to say, "Small profits can provide quick returns." Our family soon got a reputation as good mats weavers, and we were able to sell lots of them in the local markets.

Student in the Cultural Revolution

Between 1966 and 1976, many schools and universities were closed as during the Cultural Revolution many young people became Red Guards. By the beginning of the 1970s, however, it became obvious that communes needed people who could read, write, and do simple arithmetic in order to teach in their primary schools. To meet this need, some college places were opened to train teachers for the village schools. Our commune had the opportunity to send five people to be candidates for the entrance examination for college. The officials thought that I should be one of them as they said I was intelligent, hard working, and from a peasant family. They said that I was a perfect model of Mao's ideal. Baba and Mu were so excited. They knew that this meant that afterwards I could get a job as a teacher with a government salary. My status would change from that of a farmer to being a government official, I would have a city *hukou*[6] and would be better able to support the family.

I remember our family dinner the evening before the entrance examination. Mu cooked some meat which we usually only ate at festivals. At first, nobody talked about the coming examination, but I could tell that Mu was both happy and nervous about it. Finally, my younger brother, Chun asked me when I would come back after the exam. After I told him, Baba told me that I should not be nervous, but just be myself during the examination. Before I went to bed, Mu put 1 RMB in my pocket. The next day an official from our commune escorted the five candidates from our village to the college. I still remember the topic of the essay in the Chinese test: "If there is no smell of dung, the rice has no fragrance." We had to wait two weeks for the results. When the news came that I had the offer to go to college, everyone was so happy. I can't tell you how pleased I was to go as the commune's student to study at the college.

By nature, I am curious and I was eager to see the world outside. In the same way as for my junior high school, I had to take my own bedding, mats, pots, a bucket, and a vacuum flask to get hot water for washing. My parents and the commune officials made sure that I had all that I needed, including two sets of clothes. It was fashionable then for young intellectuals and students to use a pen, have a flashlight, and wear leather shoes. They were called the "small three". Baba bought me a pen and a flashlight, but he couldn't afford to buy the leather shoes. The fees were covered by the commune, and I also received 3 RMB a month. This was more money than I had ever received before.

In those days with neither air conditioning nor electric fans, during the summer the dormitories were so hot it was difficult to sleep, and in winter so cold that you could see your breath. Nevertheless, I was proud to be chosen to attend college and determined to do my very best, so that I would become a government worker with a stable salary. This was especially important as I now had three younger sisters, and two young brothers named Chun and Xia. As the oldest child, I had a special responsibility for the family until Chun married and could take over the responsibility of looking after his brothers and youngest sister. It was unusual for a daughter to have such responsibility and I was determined to fulfil my obligations.

The college was intended to train primary school teachers, but the initial group of students were of different ages and educational backgrounds. Some had finished primary school and others had graduated from junior high school or even senior high school. We studied Chinese, politics, mathematics, chemistry, music, and physical education at the level suitable for teaching primary school students. One of my favourite courses was learning to play the wind organ. Since we came from such different backgrounds, every second month we were assessed to see whether we were in the class at the most suitable level for us. One thing we all did have in common was a similar class background—we were all from poor peasant families. As food was provided for us, we all tried to save a little from our allowance of 3 RMB to take back to our families.

At weekends, we were free to go home, and initially I went home to tell my family all about what had happened during the past week. My sisters and brothers were so curious about life at college and what we studied; they would sit and listen. Chun, my first brother, was especially interested, and always asked a lot of questions. Once he said, "Jiejie (elder sister) is my model and I will study hard, so that I can have the same opportunity as she has had." That pleased me. Nevertheless, it took me four hours to walk home from the college, and the journey required that I crossed a high mountain pass through an isolated forest. Here, the wind howled through the trees sounding like a pack of wolves. The strange noises and isolated terrain frightened me, and I felt very vulnerable. Reluctantly, I decided that however much I liked going home at weekends I wouldn't go, and so I stayed in college with some of the other girls.

The daily schedule was fixed. We studied from 7:30 a.m. and finished at 10 p.m. We ate three meals a day in the college canteen, and had an hour rest at noon. Although food was free, it was still limited, so we did not play physical games as these would make us feel hungry. We only ate meat once a week; most often we were given rice, potatoes, sweet potatoes, Chinese cabbage, and radish. The planned course of study was for three years, but as there was such a shortage of primary school teachers in the villages this was shortened for us to two-and-a-half years.

Whilst I was at college, I bought some glasses to help me read. The glasses were a great help, but some of the girls started joking that they made me look like a monster with big eyes. This made me feel very self-conscious. I also thought that only scholars and city people wear glasses not a peasant girl like me. I therefore decided to stop wearing them. I put them away in my box and continued squinting at the blackboard trying to read what the teacher had written.

Each class had several Chinese Communist Party members and Communist Youth League members. They had joined the Communist Party of China (CCP) or Communist Youth League whilst in the army or in the countryside before they started college. The CCP members formed the class committee, and each class also had a Youth League branch. To become a member of the Communist Youth League a student had to submit an application to the class branch. They would consider the application in terms of the applicant's daily performance and then write a brief report to the College Youth League Committee. To be accepted as a member of the Communist Youth League one had to have a good all-round performance and be knowledgeable in political ideology. The secretary of the Youth League branch was a roommate of mine and she often talked with me about how I should become a member of the Communist Youth League. I finally decided to become a member. When I told my parents of my decision, they were both pleased because they considered this showed how much I was appreciated at college. When the time came, I made my vows to serve my country and the CCP with some of my fellow students.[7]

During my time at college, I not only progressed in my studies, but also made friends with others on my course. One young man in particular became interested in me and asked me to go on a date with him. At this time, to be invited on a date was a serious matter as it implied that you were willing to commit to marriage. When I talked the matter over with Mu she did not think it was a good idea because the young man lived in another county, and if I were to marry him I would have to live with his family. Our family would therefore lose a major contributor to its income while some of the children were still young. I struggled with this advice as I liked the young man, and even though he had not said anything, I could tell he liked me. But, I had four sisters and two brothers all of whom were at school and Mu was pregnant again. Baba and Mu needed my support so how could I desert the family at such a crucial time? I had to tell him that our relationship couldn't continue. When the course came to an end, we had to part. We were both very sad when I returned to Jin'e and my family.

At that time, when students graduated we each wrote a letter to the other students on our course to encourage them in their future work. These letters were filled with the patriotic fervour that was common during the Cultural Revolution. I got one letter saying, "Let us struggle and work together for the cause of Communism. Let us work for the happiness and well-being of the Proletariat." Other letters said: "Be loyal to the Party's education development and be a student of the people for ever"; "We wish you well in your future post to follow Chairman Mao's revolutionary line and move forward"; "I hope you will make a new contribution to the education front for the Party"; "Do your best in your new job with your whole heart to serve the people, and work hard for the Party." This was indeed my ambition.

Village Teacher

In 1975, when I was 22 years old, I began working as a teacher in the small school in the village of Heping (和平 literally "Peaceful") which had a population of about 3000 people. Villages usually consisted of a number of large clans with the same family name. This was the case in Heping where the three main families were the Ai, the Li, and the Ma. A member of the Ai family was the village Party Secretary and a member of the Li family was the village head; they were the most important figures in the village.

The little school in Heping previously had no qualified teacher, only five secondary school graduates who were supported by the villagers. They were known as "substitute teachers", a term used for anyone who worked in rural schools without formal qualifications. Substitute teachers had little status and earned little money. When I joined the school, there were then six substitute teachers, one for each of the six grades. The substitute teachers got a salary of 5 RMB per month and the villagers gave them some land to grow vegetables. Because I was a qualified teacher, I got 31 RMB per month and 15.5 kg of rice. This was a considerable income at the time. Students paid 2.5 RMB for tuition annually, but some parents were so poor they couldn't pay the fees. As I was responsible for the school's finances, the officials compensated for these unpaid tuition fees by deducting the money from my salary. I didn't complain about this for several years because I knew that my salary was much higher than that of the substitute teachers and I wanted to keep in good relations with them. Even though I urged the parents to pay in cash, some could only pay the school fees in sweet potatoes. As I received a lot of sweet potatoes, I shared them with my family.

As Jin'e was only an hour walk away I went home every Sunday to help take care of my younger brothers and sisters. At this time, three articles were considered to be fashionable possessions: a watch, a sewing machine, and a radio. All were expensive, and my family wasn't able to afford them. So I used my first three months' salary to buy a watch, which was popular with government officials. Next I wanted to buy a sewing machine for my sister, Shi, who was not interested in studying so we planned to send her to study tailoring. However, with my poor eye-sight, I was often afraid of the journey; in summer it was the danger of snakes, and in winter of slipping on the ice.

I was the only teacher at the school who knew Pinyin, the official system for Standard Chinese in Roman lettering.[8] My responsibility was to teach the first-year students who were seven or eight years old; they had no experience of school life or of the discipline required. As they were only used to playing in the fields or doing simple jobs at home, they found it difficult to sit still for very long and some of them were very naughty. Some of the students had nits in their hair, and fleas were common in the children's clothes. I needed to be patient with these first-time students as I tried to teach them numbers and basic arithmetic. I continually asked them not to be late, to listen in class, to review their studies after class, and to finish their homework. I tried my best to use simple and vivid stories based on what they knew in their daily-life and encouraged them to speak out in class by asking them questions. I also taught them how to write some of the Chinese characters and even a little music.

It was hard, but I liked teaching these first-year students, and seeing them gradually becoming interested in learning. Children in the grades above third grade usually had a week off in March and October so they could help their families plant and harvest the crops. The village gave an area of land to the school so that teachers could grow different types of crops. We could then sell some of these, and with the money, we would buy some meat and noodles. In those days, it was a luxury to eat noodles with meat. Every two months, we teachers had a meal together to relax and enjoy some free time together. Rural schools in China then were supported by local villagers. If any practical work needed to be done, local people would do it, repairing windows and painting walls. Sometimes the older children would go into the hills to collect stones that could be used to make concrete for the buildings and playground. Over the years, I came to know all the young people in the village and their parents, and eventually saw them grow up, marry, and have children of their own.

Usually I would work at school in the morning; in the afternoons, I visited local families to encourage them to send their daughters as well as their sons to school. Parents often sent their sons even when they were as young as four, but kept their daughters at home doing housework until they were as old as eight. I used to argue with the parents that if they did not send the girls to school, when they grew up they would not even be able to read their own name. If the parents said that they couldn't afford to send both daughters and sons to school, I went to the local officials to ask for help. Eventually, the officials agreed that parents need only pay one-third of the school fees before the child started school and the remaining two-thirds sometime in the future. Often the parents did not pay, so the officials once again deducted the fees from my salary.

On occasions a soldier would come to teach at our school. These soldiers had returned home from the army, and were sent to the same teacher training college where I had studied. Most of them were peasants with little previous schooling, but because of their military achievements and membership of the Party, their political thought was considered advanced. They were therefore only given a three-month training course before being sent to teach in rural schools. Former soldiers were considered to be good models for the future of the country, and were highly respected in the community. In practice, they knew little about arithmetic or the Chinese language, which sometimes led to embarrassing situations that today seem quite comical.

For example, on one occasion a soldier-teacher was teaching basic arithmetic at a nearby primary school. He told the students that 1 kg equals three times 500 grams. One of the children eventually built up enough courage to say that his Dad had told him that 1 kg equals two times 500 grams. The soldier-teacher looked at him and after a pause said, "Your father is right because his is a small kilogramme whilst mine is a large kilogramme." A teacher in another village school took this further and said that there are two sorts of kilogram weights: a large kilogram equal to three 500 grams and a small kilogram equal to two 500 grams!

When it came to the Chinese lessons, similar situations occurred. Chinese characters are usually made up of two or more parts called radicals. For example, the character "good" 好 (Pinyin *hao*) is made of two radicals, one meaning woman 女 (*nu*) and the other son 子 (*zi*). Taken together the radicals are pronounced *hao* while taken separately they are pronounced *nu zi*. On one occasion, I remember a soldier-teacher was getting the students to learn one of the revolutionary sayings common at that time—忠心耿耿—*loyal and devoted, faithful and true*, which means to work wholeheartedly. Instead of reading this as *zhongxin-genggeng* he took the *geng* 耿 as two radicals *er* 耳 meaning "ear" and *huo* 火 meaning "fire". So instead of telling the students to say *geng geng* he was telling them to say *er huo er huo*, which made the slogan to mean "loyal and devoted, ear fire, ear fire". When I heard the students loudly chanting this in the classroom next door, I was shocked, and then I realized what the problem was. I had to take great care in dealing with the problem as all the soldier-teachers were highly respected, and if I shamed him in any way I could get into trouble which would influence my career. So, with great humility I entered the classroom and explained that Chinese is complicated and these characters could also have a different pronunciation. In this case, they would be pronounced *geng* meaning "faithful and true". Fortunately, the soldier-teacher merely nodded his approval at the revolutionary saying. I quietly bowed to the soldier-teacher and withdrew from the classroom.

Baba had an especially good friend who had an adopted son called Ze. During the Cultural Revolution Ze was working in a neighbouring village, but on his day off he would often come to Jin'e. When his coat was torn or he needed his clothes altered he often asked our family for help, and Mu would ask me to do the task. In this way, I got to know him. In 1974, Ze and his step-father visited Mu and Baba, and after chatting for a while, Ze's step-father suggested that Ze and I should marry. Baba was quiet, but Mu was angered by the suggestion; she said they should not have come directly to them, but should have gone through a matchmaker. Ze's step-father apologized and quietly left the house. Later, he appointed a matchmaker, but Mu did not like her and sent her away. He then found another matchmaker, and this time Mu was happy with her.[9]

Ze was an only child, didn't have any brothers or sisters to look after, and would inherit his parent's property in the city. Baba thought that Ze was a suitable prospect as he had an urban *hukou* and a salaried job at the commune stall. Baba also knew that he was a hard worker and got along well with my sisters and brothers. He was also strong and tall. Nevertheless, I said that I would prefer to wait a couple of years before getting married as I had only just started teaching. To be honest, I still liked the young man from college. Baba reminded me of an old proverb, "When a big man falls, much grass is flattened," which means that "He is a strong and healthy man." With our positions in the commune, Ze and I would both get food supplied by the government; such a marriage would therefore be advantageous to the family as a whole. With some sadness, I decided to forget about my student friend and I married Ze.

Notes

1. Lei Feng (18 December 1940–15 August 1962) was a soldier in the People's Liberation Army who become a legend in Communist China. After his death, Lei was portrayed as a selfless and modest person devoted to the Communist Party, Mao Zedong, and the people of China. In 1963, he

became the subject of a nationwide propaganda campaign, "Follow the examples of Comrade Lei Feng."
2. The Young Pioneers of China is a youth organization for children aged six to fourteen run by the Communist Youth League, an organization of older youth that itself comes under the Communist Party of China.
3. See note 13 Chap. 1.
4. The term "Four Olds" (四旧; pinyin: sì jiù) first appeared on 1 June 1966, in an editorial in the People's Daily newspaper written by Chen Boda entitled "Sweep Away All Monsters and Demons."
5. Literally, this means "the great trend of going abroad".
6. *Hukou* is a record of a government system of household regulation that determines where citizens are allowed to live.
7. To join the Communist Party Youth League (CPYL) the applicant has to be between 14 and 28. The Communist Party oath of admission is as follows: "It is my will to join the Communist Party of China, uphold the Party's programme, observe the provisions of the Party Constitution, fulfil a Party member's duties, carry out the Party's decisions, strictly observe Party discipline, guard Party secrets, be loyal to the Party, work hard, fight for communism throughout my life, be ready at all times to sacrifice my all for the Party and the people, and never betray the Party."
8. This was published by the Government in 1958.
9. Matchmaking was considered to be a skilful task. The matchmaker should not only be familiar with the families of both the man and woman but also be able to understand the strengths and weaknesses of their situations.

CHAPTER 3

Ze's Story: Husband of First Daughter

My eldest sister was born 20 years before me in 1930 during the Republican period of China. My mother's second child died when he was only one-year old, her third and fourth children were girls, born in 1934 and 1939, and her fifth, a son, was born in 1943. The birth of the sixth, a girl born in 1945, led the family having to take a very hard decision. Because the family was very poor, our parents knew that another mouth to feed would threaten the survival of their four living children. They sent the other children out of the house to play, and then filled a bucket with water and immersed the newborn girl in the water. This harsh decision was one that many poor families had to make in those days. Daughters were killed because as soon as a girl was old enough she was married off and went to live and work with her husband's family. I, the seventh child, was born in 1950—the year after the People's Republic of China was established.

At this time Baba, the eldest son of my grandpa, was the headman of the village. Grandpa was a famous lawyer in our locality, so Baba had a good education and read many books. Many people liked Grandpa, but some people who felt that he had not treated them justly disliked him, and this was to cause our family problems in the future. Baba's youngest brother worked in the local police station. Baba told me that in 1948, this youngest uncle hid a Communist Party member who was being hunted by the Republican forces to avoid capture. After the Communist Party took over rule of the country, this man was made Director of Public Security for the entire county. My uncle was appointed regional head of security by him. However, during the Land Reform period, my uncle confiscated some belongings of a landlord and took them back to his own home. Grandma started using some of these things. A few months later, this was discovered by people who disliked Grandpa, and they used this as evidence that his family should be classified as "rich peasants". Soon after, the Communist Party of China (CCP) ruled that there were five classes of people considered as bad: landowners, rich peasants, counter-revolutionaries, bad members, and rightists. They were discriminated against and oppressed in many ways. For example, people in these classes had to do heavy manual work for which they didn't get any work-points and didn't even have the right to attend village meetings. My elder brother also got caught up in all of these problems so that even though he had an excellent score in primary school, he was not allowed to go on to junior high school. Though decades have passed, I still remember how sad and disappointed he was when he was refused by the school. Baba wrote lots of letters of complaint about this injustice, but they were rejected by the commune leader because he also had a personal grudge against my family.

Like many districts of China, ours was transformed by the Communist Government's directive in 1959 to form Peoples' Communes, and was also badly affected by the famine of 1958–60. In 1960, when food was in desperately short supply, my mother became sick with emphysema; because she had been so hungry, she had eaten a kind of white clay. While recovering in hospital she was given a bowl of rice every day, but she would often sneak it outside and give it to me as I was not allowed into the hospital. Since she ate no food, her health gradually got worse and the day she left hospital she was too weak to walk home. After two days, she was so hungry that she asked for a bowl of soup, but nothing was available at home. I clearly remember how weak and thin she was when she died. I sometimes think that if we had had a single bowl of soup that day, Mom might have lived longer and could have survived the famine. Maybe she would even be alive today like Grandma Zhen.

Before the famine, it was the custom to take a corpse up to a tomb in the nearby hills, but during the famine, nobody had enough strength to build such tombs. They merely took the corpse into the hills and covered it with mud and stones to protect it from the wild animals. When my mother died my father, my elder brother, and the three sons-in-law, all tried to carry her corpse. Even though she had been very thin, they were all weak so they could only manage to carry her a short distance before they needed to sit and rest. Finally, the five men stopped on the road as they realized it was impossible for them to carry the body all the way to the top of the hill. Reluctantly they decided to find a spot by the road, where they covered the body with mud and stones. Years later I heard a fortune-teller say that the place they had chosen was in fact one with a good *feng shui*.[1] When she died, I was nine years old.

I continued living with my father for a while, as Baba did not have a wife anymore and I no longer had a mum. Baba sewed a little pocket into my poor clothes so that if I found any scrap of food I could hide it and bring it home. Occasionally, I did find a root, small vegetables, and even insects like crickets. Some of our neighbours were so desperately hungry that they, like my mum, ate white clay, but it caused terrible stomach pains, and if the mud didn't pass through the stomach, the person died. I remember once after eating some of the mud I couldn't shit and had to have it manually pulled out. Those were terrible days. You don't know what it was like to be so hungry.

During the famine, I was a student at the local primary school. The winter was bitterly cold that year, and as my clothes were so thin and I didn't have any shoes, I couldn't stop shaking. I decided to stay at home, but I didn't tell my father as I knew that he would be angry. Then one day the teacher complained to him and asked him why I didn't go to school. Baba was angry with me, but he couldn't do anything as we had little food and no clothes. It was at this time that his brother, my youngest uncle, got his job back and suggested that he adopt me as his son.

My youngest uncle married in 1949. His wife came from a wealthy family in Chongqing and had previously been married to my oldest uncle who was a battalion commander and had fought in the war with Japan. When the army was in Chongqing, they met, fell in love, and married. All her family members had died during the war, so they planned to return to his village which was several hundred kilometres away, have a quiet life and many children. Her husband had two unmarried younger brothers—my father and this youngest uncle. She lived with her husband, his two brothers, and parents-in-law, and worked hard to learn the local customs, and gradually became integrated into the family. In the first year, life was peaceful; she helped her mother-in-law with the housework and farmed the fields with the men. She was looking forward to having a baby which was her greatest wish, but then in the winter of 1948 the unexpected happened.

Because uncle had been a battalion commander, he was highly respected by the villagers, and became involved in local politics including an ongoing conflict between my grandfather and some of the local people. He soon became hated by one of the landowners because he intervened in his lawsuit against my grandfather. The landowner was determined to get rid of uncle. One night there was a robbery, and one of the robbers is said to have shouted out my uncle's name. When the police heard of this, they immediately went to arrest my uncle. At the time, a county head had the right to execute thieves. The landowner bribed the county head so that when the policeman reported the details of the case to him, he agreed to execute uncle that very night. He was worried that if he didn't do this straightaway the police might not find sufficient evidence to convict him especially considering my grandfather's reputation. So uncle was shot and killed. Grandpa was deeply upset and refused to bury his son's body. He put the body on a bed of charcoal and covered it with fine river sand. He kept his son's body like this until the landowner was executed during the land reforms in 1949. At the sound of the gun shot, Grandpa knelt on the ground and cried, "My dear son, I finally have avenged you." He buried his son's body on the same day as the landowner was buried.

After her beloved husband was killed, auntie was desperate and wanted to kill herself. Everyone she had ever loved was dead; life seemed hopeless. She then realized she was pregnant and started feeling the baby moving within her. After a few months, her mother-in-law asked her if she would consider marrying her brother-in-law, that is, my youngest uncle. Auntie didn't know what to do. She could not return to her home town as she had no living relatives. She knew that her brother-in-law was a kind man, so she accepted the suggestion and married him. After the marriage, she was surprised to find that he often went out late at night. She was curious about what he did, so one night she followed him and found out that he was part of a local underground communist group. When the Communist Party came to power in 1949, my uncle got a job in the government because of his contribution to the Party in previous years.

Sadly, auntie lost the baby in the sixth month. After this, she became pregnant on two more occasions, but both children died soon after birth. My uncle offered to adopt me. Baba was at first reluctant as he hoped to look after me himself. He learnt that I hadn't been attending school because I was hungry and cold, so he accepted the suggestion especially as uncle now had a government job in the county town.

City Boy

I was ten when I went to live with my uncle. I still remember the day Baba took me to my uncle's house. After mum died, Baba and I always went everywhere together. After lunch with my uncle, he was going to leave, but as I stood up my steps were stopped by the look in his eyes. I was sad but said nothing. Looking at father's receding figure in the street, my eyes were full of tears.

I missed my family, and I didn't like living in a strange house in what was for me a big town. To be honest, the conditions were much better than at home because I had food to eat, but everything was so different from what I was used to. At weekends, I wanted to visit my family even though Baba said that I shouldn't come back. Nevertheless, I often made the three-hour walk along the narrow single-track road to the village. At first, my sister beat me with a whip and shouted at me saying I should go back to the town. Even as she beat me I could see tears in her eyes, and I knew she understood how much I missed them. I think she was worried that uncle would change his mind and send me back. Then, one day when I returned to them, I found everything strangely silent. When I opened the door, I saw the house was empty; no-one was living there anymore. They had all gone! I looked for some food, but there was none there. Tears ran down my face as I realized that this part of my life was over; I had to stay with uncle in the town.

Although I didn't realize it at the time, my adoption was a major benefit for me. Because my uncle was a city official I now had a city *hukou*[2] that allowed me not only to live in the city but to study at a city school. I studied in the town primary school where the class size was only about 20 students compared to 30 or more in village schools. The teachers were nice and professional, and I began enjoying school. I tried to do my best in my studies and often came at the top of the class in the exams. I was even appointed the person who stood at the front of the whole school to lead the morning broadcast gymnastics. It was a great honour for a village boy like me to lead city children, but then one morning something very funny happened. I can laugh about it now, but at the time, I was so embarrassed. I was at the front leading the morning exercises when the rope I used as a belt snapped, and my trousers fell to the ground in front of the whole school. I quickly pulled them up and tried dutifully to continue with the remainder of the exercises. I remember how the students laughed! I made a make-shift belt from some rice straws to hold my trousers up for the rest of the day.

During term time, I would get up early to cook breakfast for myself before going to school. Lessons started at 8 a.m. and lasted until 3 p.m. after which we played with the other children in the school playground. One of our favourite games was *zhuifengzi* (literally "chasing madman"). In this game, we would divide into two groups; one group were the madmen and the others tried to catch them. Once a madman was touched he was no longer a madman and immediately started chasing other madmen. When all the madmen had been touched, the game finished. The game was good because it required no equipment, and on cold days, the exercise made us warm. In those days, we didn't have many toys, not like children today who have lots of things to play with.

We did however have a table-tennis table made from concrete and a set of bats. One day every year, the school organized a ping-pong team and gave the team members some training. In 1963, when I was 13, I was lucky enough to be selected by the coach who thought I had talent. I went on to become the school ping-pong champion, and had the chance to compete with champions from other schools. Every week the coach would train me, and I steadily improved. By 1965, when I was 15, I became champion of all the schools in the city. As I was recognized as a junior athlete, I could have had the opportunity to train to become a professional ping-pong athlete.

At the weekends, I did some work to help support my family just as all the other children did; I carried water and washed clothes. I also did jobs like cutting grass for the cattle and carrying coal so as to earn some pocket money. It was hard work, but I didn't mind. We were continually being told that we must work to eat, and, as I wanted to eat, I worked.

Red Guard

It was in May 1966, when I was 16 that the dramatic political change we call the "Cultural Revolution" began. Chairman Mao Zedong at the age of 72 swam the Yangtze River to set us a good example by his strength and vigour. Many of us students wanted to be strong like him. Then, we began to hear news that in Beijing students were organizing themselves into groups called Red Guards. In the general excitement, normal school routine began to break down. The Red Guards organized mass rallies in Tiananmen Square where they affirmed the revolutionary teaching of Chairman Mao by waving their copies of the "Little Red Book". We all became so excited at this news. It appealed to our desire for revolution and, to be honest, our sense of teenage rebellion.

In August and September of that year, we learned that the Red Guards were committing themselves to destroying the "Four Olds" and cultivating the "Four New". The "Four Olds" were Old Customs, Old Culture, Old Habits, and Old Ideas, whilst the "Four New" things were New Customs, New Culture, New Habits, and New Ideas. Groups of Red Guards made speeches, fixed posters onto walls, and harassed intellectuals because they were considered to be committed to the "Four Olds". They even entered temples, knocked over statues of the bodhisattvas, and smashed cultural relics. They also raided homes looking for "reactionary materials", which included old phonographs, religious items, and even books of the teaching of Confucius. They destroyed these books, and told the people that they should only read books by Chairman Mao. In some homes, people had a god-shelf on which they had statues of their family gods, and a memorial tablet with the names of their ancestors. The Red Guards also smashed these and warned the families not to make any more offerings to them.

I heard that in Beijing the Red Guards even attacked pedestrians who they considered to be wearing western style clothes or had western hair styles. These things were thought to be bourgeoisie and show revisionist trends that had to be destroyed if the new China was to be built. Young people were not allowed to speak of love, which was regarded as a bourgeoisie ideology that had no place in a Socialist China. This all sounds so strange to the students of today. Can you imagine what this current generation would do without their nice clothes and cell phones? How things have changed in 50 years!

When my classes came to an end in the summer of 1966, I spent my time reading the writings of Chairman Mao, and discussing what they meant with my friends. That autumn, those who wanted to join the struggle in Beijing and other major cities were given free rail travel. Some of the older boys formed themselves into groups and went off to Beijing, but as I was one of the youngest, I went to the nearby city of Chongqing with a group of younger students. My step-parents did not oppose my trip because it was something that young people were doing right across the country. They just asked me to take care and look after myself. I didn't really know what we would be doing so I didn't take any luggage with me, not even any spare clothes. The school however, had given us some money for our time with the Red Guards. When we arrived in Chongqing we marched through the city proclaiming revolution, but we didn't beat anybody like in some of the other cities. In fact, the majority of us never beat anyone nor damaged any buildings. It was more like an exciting adventure during which we were for the first time in our lives able to travel to a big city. All the schools in Chongqing were turned into Red Guard reception stations, and I lived in one of these. The authorities put mats and quilts on the desks and we slept there, often more than ten of us sleeping in each classroom. During the day I wandered around the city with my group, and at night we returned to the school. Accommodation was free and we didn't even have to pay for the food.

Then some of us lost contact with the larger group and soon we ran out of money. The novelty of the adventure began to fade, and it was all becoming rather boring. We were also missing our families, so after a month we decided to go home. On our way home, we stopped at the prefectural city, where we found that we could stay at the Party hotel. We were offered free food and accommodation, and as we were not required to do any work, we decided to stay for a while. Time passed, and one day when I was chatting to a waiter, he mentioned that the following week was Chinese New Year. We had all completely forgotten what date it was, and we quickly decided to go back home and enjoy the nice foods on offer at this holiday time. My own clothes had also become quite dirty and I was beginning to have lice. So, I returned home after the adventure. I was then 17 years old and I must admit that I was really pleased to be back.

A few months later the central government stopped allowing Red Guards to go to Beijing. By summer the excitement of the students had waned and groups of Red Guards even started fighting each other. Nevertheless, revolutionary ideas still continued in our town. One of our neighbours had previously worked at a university in Beijing. He and his wife were both English majors and they occasionally talked to each other in English in order to practise their spoken English. One day some Red Guards heard them talking in a foreign language and, thinking that they must be counter-revolutionaries reported them to the authorities. Both of them were dragged into the streets and publicly criticized.

As all the high schools were closed, I stayed at home during the rest of the year but, through various contacts of my step-father, I got a job as a guard for a commune vegetable garden. As food was still limited, some people would steal the vegetables and my job was to catch anyone trying to steal them. However, as people usually stole the vegetables at night and I only worked during the daytime, I didn't catch a single thief! In my spare time, I used to carry water, coal, and the yellow mud which my family mixed with coal as a fuel for cooking.

In 1969, the Ninth Congress of the Communist Party announced that the Party had been purged and that only loyal Maoists were in high positions. City youth were ordered to go to the countryside to be educated by the peasants.[3] The government gave each of us 230 RMB to support us the whole time we lived in the villages. I was sent to a village not far from my home. The villagers allocated me a small thatched cottage, about 25 square metres. It had a kitchen with a stove, a water tank, a bucket, a cupboard, a square table, and a long bench and a bedroom with a narrow little bed. The cottage had a small window with a little table placed under it. Here I could sit and read, but even in the daytime the room was dark. I used to get up early in the morning, fetch a couple of buckets of water from the well and cook a pot of food that I would eat throughout the day. During the day, we worked on the farmland and were given rice and corn according to how much we worked alongside the local famers. The commune headquarters was in the town and I sometimes had to go there to attend meetings. When I was in the town, I would buy salt to make the rice and corn tasty.

Together with the other students, I spent two evenings every week studying the ideology of Chairman Mao. But, with no books apart from the Little Red Book, and no amusements such as radio or TV, the only thing we did in the evenings was sleep. The nights were quiet; all you could hear were the sound of birds and insects. Many of the city students found their time in the countryside really hard as they didn't like the smelly toilets and the poor food. Some were not strong enough to work in the fields and sometimes they couldn't understand what the peasants were saying because of their strong accent.

Although many of the city students struggled with life in the village, because I had grown up in a village I quickly adapted and integrated with the villagers. I was appointed as the leader of a group of ten educated youths or *zhi qing* as we were called, and with my city *hukou* I was able to buy rice cheaply, so the peasants were happy to welcome us to any village feast. My step-father had told me to work hard as this would open good work opportunities in the future. I did just what he said and won the praise of the commune officials.

The city youths decided to set up a performance group to promote the Party's policies. As I got on well with both the villagers and the city youth, I was made the leader of the team. We used many ideas we had learned from the Peking Opera, and every two months, we held a performance in the school playground that was much enjoyed by the whole village. We also learned to dance; one of the dances we performed was the Loyalty Dance, so called because its steps followed the shape of the Chinese character for loyalty. All the songs accompanying the dances were about Chairman Mao. We also had to learn some of the famous quotations of Chairman Mao, so the first thing we did every morning was read his "Little Red Book". By the end of their time in the village, some students were able to recite the whole book. I was sometimes asked to give a speech in the commune's simple theatre mainly because I had a good memory and spoke clearly. It was actually quite an honour.

Every time I went to the commune office, I would pop in to have a meal with Cheng and Zhen. My step-father knew them, so it was easy for me to visit them. If my clothes were torn or I needed something, I could always ask them for help. When I first got to know them in 1969 there were six children in the family. I liked them a lot, as they were hard working and kind. That's when I met Shun.

I worked in the village for three years until 1971 when the government policy changed. City students were then able to return home, and some were even recommended to study at college. I was twice recommended for college, but on both occasions, I was not accepted. The official said that somebody had reported that the background of my step-father was complicated and so they were against me being accepted. My step-father said he might have offended some people from his work. Preference was given to students from poor peasant families like Zhen's, so I was not accepted. I was very disappointed as I really thought I would be given the chance, but it was not to be.

In 1973, with the help of a friend of my step-father, I was given a job at the commune shop and was paid 21 RMB a month, which was a good salary then. At that time, all daily supplies were controlled by the Planned Economy, and I was responsible for selling items such as kerosene, sugar, oil, noodles, eggs, and meat in the commune store. Ever since 1955, food tickets had been given to rural people and these had become part of our daily life.[4] Pork, beef, mutton, eggs, sugar, brown sugar, cakes, and noodles were rationed and could only be bought in limited amounts. I remember when the rations were 0.5 kg of meat and two eggs per person per month. Watches, bicycles, and sewing machines were rare luxuries, and only a limited number of tickets for them were sent to each unit and people took turns to get them.

After a couple of years, my step-father suggested that I should consider marrying Shun. I was happy with this suggestion as I liked her. My step-father therefore approached Cheng and Zhen, but they rejected the proposal saying that he should do things properly by going through a matchmaker. So this is what he did and the marriage arrangements began.

Ze Marries Shun

It was then the custom that the girl's parents gave a gift to the couple. Although Cheng was still poor, he managed to buy wood from different friends, and had two cupboards made as our wedding gift. The wedding was a simple affair. Shun and I went to the commune leader to get permission to marry, and then our families had dinner together. The following day Shun and I moved some of her belongings to my small house.

That year Shun also started as a teacher at the school in Heping village. As both of us were new to the village, it was important for us to build good relations with the village leaders. One of the local customs was that on the village leader's birthday the villagers would give him a gift. This usually amounted to only 1 RMB, but as Shun was a new staff member at the school, she gave him 3 RMB. In this way, we sought to integrate into the village and be accepted by them.

1976 is an important year in the history of China. In January, Prime Minister Zhou Enlai died. He had survived the purges of top officials during the Cultural Revolution, and was the main driving force behind the affairs of state during much of that time. He tried to mitigate the damage caused by the Red Guards and to protect some of the other top officials. In 1973, he also brought Deng Xiaoping back into the Party leadership at the tenth Party Congress and struggled against the "Gang of Four".[5] When he died, the whole country, top officials, ordinary people, his friends and even his former enemies were sad. There was a massive public outpouring of grief in Beijing that turned into anger against the "Gang of Four".

Later that year, on the afternoon of September 9, the radio presenter announced that Chairman Mao Zedong had died. Within an hour, everyone in the village had heard the news; we decided to hold a commemoration that would last several days. In the village school, a black curtain was draped across the wall, and a large portrait of Chairman Mao hung in the middle. Around the portrait, nine characters declared "Chairman Mao Zedong has an eternal life," and on both sides, mortuary scrolls were hung. On September 18 in Beijing's Tiananmen Square, a great memorial service was held; our village also held a memorial service when the people wept loudly. Hua Guofeng succeeded him. He was determined to follow all the principles established by Chairman Mao, so in 1977, he set out what was known as "Hua Guofeng grasps the principles to govern the country."[6]

It was a time when many of the malpractices that had occurred in the communes were examined and offenders were punished and lost their jobs. Also at this time, a young woman who was a *Zhi qing* and on good terms with the Secretary of the local Communist Party started coming daily to my stall to buy kerosene. Shun and I thought this was unfair as it meant that there was little kerosene left in the stall for the peasants to buy. As she was probably hoarding the fuel, I decided to restrict the amount I sold to her. This annoyed her and she wrote a letter to the officials criticizing my management of the commune stall. This was something that the authorities could not ignore.

One of Shun's friends told her that some officials were coming to investigate my accounts. Shun was afraid because she knew what trouble this could cause. I told her that all my accounts were correct and there was nothing for her to fear. Before the investigation, Shun helped me to check carefully the accounts once again. The officials who came were of low peasant status and were determined to be rigorous in carrying out their investigation. When they first arrived Shun invited them to have a meal with us, but they refused because they did not want to give any hint that they had been bribed. The leading official told Shun, "Even though we grew up together we will carry out the investigation thoroughly." Shun replied, "I totally understand and I will fully comply." They carefully examined all my accounts and only when they were assured that they were in order were they willing to eat with us. The leader of the investigators reported to the commune that I was a good and responsible young man. Shun was so pleased that I had been proved to be innocent of any wrongdoing, that Zhen made a pair of shoes for my leader as a gift. Shoes are a special gift particularly when they are made by hand because they are made of thousands of stitches, which expresses the idea of being thankful a thousand times over.[7]

On 6 October 1976, just a month after Mao's death, Deng Xiaoping, led other top officials to depose the "Gang of Four" from power. This marked the end of the Cultural Revolution and the beginning of a new era under the leadership of Deng Xiaoping which opened my life, and those of many others, to new and exciting prospects for the future.

Two years after our marriage, Shun became pregnant with our first child. She had a complicated labour, which took three days, but we were so fortunate that there was a qualified doctor in the village. He seems to have broken some regulation in the city and was punished by being sent to work in a rural hospital. In fact, both he and his wife were doctors and were able to help with the birth, although all they had was iodine as a disinfectant and an ordinary sewing needle to stitch the wound. At birth, the baby had stopped breathing, but they managed to resuscitate the little boy. The long birth left Shun exhausted. As the doctors had no medicines, Zhen got some traditional Chinese medicine that they could give Shun. It took a couple of weeks for her to recover, and thankfully, the baby was strong and healthy.

Initially Cheng and Zhen said they couldn't help with the baby, but they were so excited that he was a boy they wanted to ensure great care was taken of him. As he was the firstborn of the third generation, Grandpa Luo who helped to look after Shun and other children used his savings to buy a big chicken and duck to eat, which at that time was a big gift. From the very next day after the birth, friends started coming to congratulate us, bringing with them gifts of eggs, rice, and even a clothes ticket or a 2 RMB note. We cooked the eggs and rice to feed our kind friends.

It was a common practice in our area for the mother's family to find an auspicious day soon after the birth of a child for all the family members to come together.[8] Zhen's family set this as being seven days after the birth, and some 30 relatives came, bringing gifts they carried on shoulder poles. They brought gifts of clothes, chickens, noodles, pork, carrying straps and other things. I had never seen so many gifts! We named the boy Jiang. From the time of my adoption I had had little contact with my three sisters, not only because they were much older than I was but also as they lived some distance away. Although they were unable to come to the celebration, they did send us gifts with my step-father. However, he neither delivered the gifts nor told us about them. Only much later when one of my sisters asked if we had received the gifts did we guess what had happened. Shun and I were angry that my step-father had deceived us in this way. It wasn't just a matter of the gifts themselves, but they showed that although I had been separated from my sisters for all these years, they still loved me, and accepted my wife and child.

Although we were really pleased with having a child, we had to face up to some new problems. Shun had 56 days of maternity leave, but who would look after the baby when that period came to an end? Shun and I both had full-time jobs that we needed to earn money. We found a lady living in Heping who was willing to be Jiang's nanny. She was 53 years old and the head of the ladies' group in the village. We paid her 10 RMB a month. We have kept a close relationship with her ever since. Jiang always had a good appetite, so we were delighted when Shun got a government registration card that gave us 5 RMB a month towards feeding the boy. Milk powder and sugar were still rationed at the time, but because both Shun and I had salaried jobs, we were able to afford to buy all the food we needed as well as to pay the nanny.

A year later Zhen and Cheng insisted that they could look after the boy, but only if Jiang lived with them in Jin'e. Shun and I considered they had sufficient means to be able to do this and as they could also have the nanny fee to support them, we agreed to their suggestion. It was very hard for Shun when Jiang was taken to Jin'e to live with her parents, but when he was old enough to go to primary school, he returned to Heping and attended the school where Shun taught. We were all happy to be reunited.

In 1979, the government introduced the one-child policy in order to curb the rapidly growing population. This restriction did have many benefits such as providing better access to education and healthcare to families that followed the rule. Shun and I decided that we would follow the Party directive and not have any more children.

A couple of years later however we faced a great dilemma. It began like this. Some local farmers were helping to build an extra dormitory to Shun's school. One of the farmers was known to be something of a fortune-teller, and he predicted that Shun would soon have a second child. As we had been taking precautions, Shun discounted this as mere superstition, but four months later she realized she was pregnant; we were both shocked. As we had government jobs this could cause us to lose our jobs and their benefits, so the only option seemed to be for Shun to have an abortion. Then Shun remembered an old classmate from her college whose husband was a doctor, and thought that she should discuss our problem with them. Shun quietly went to see the doctor. He said that at the moment the policy was not being strictly followed in the countryside, and that she should delay reporting the pregnancy until it became obvious. In fact many women did not have an abortion unless the pregnancy was reported to the authorities by someone. As the policy only covered pregnancies up to six months, some women sought to hide their condition for as long as they could. It was January and we still wore thick coats so it was not too difficult. Shun's pregnancy was noted by colleagues in the fourth month so she went to see the doctor again. He told her to delay coming to see him for another two months. Shun continued working at the school, and found various excuses to delay the date to go to the hospital. When she finally saw the doctor again, he reported that her pregnancy was in the sixth month and so the abortion could not be carried out. Three months later, a lovely little girl was born to us. We invited Jiang's former nanny to look after her, so that Shun could return to work. This is why both our son and daughter call this nanny "Grandma". Even after many years, our daughter would always go to see her when she returned home from university. The lady died in 2006 and our daughter cried all the time when we took grandma's body to the tomb. This was the first time she had experienced the death of someone she loved: that is always hard!

Another of the new policies introduced by the Party was "Reform and Opening-up", which by 1982 began to affect our village. In the early 1980s, the staff of the commune store were dismissed, and each of us was given 300 RMB as a subsidy for the future. I needed to find a new job. As there was no other shop in the village, I discussed with Shun the possibility of opening my own shop. At this time, however, government policy was not clear as to how and where people could start their own businesses. It looked as though the government was moving in the direction of allowing individuals to start their own businesses, but there were no specific regulations. We decided to open a shop but remained prepared for the possibility that the authorities might ask us to close it. If they asked us to stop we would stop, but if not we would continue.

I opened my first shop in the village school, and since it was the only shop in the village and conveniently located, I was doing good business. Eventually, the policy was clarified, which gave new opportunities for enterprising people. I decided to open a clothes shop too in Jin'e, and soon that business began growing. I could see that the new policies were going to bring great changes to our country, and was excited by the possibilities they could offer our family.

Notes

1. *Feng shui* is a Chinese philosophical system of harmonizing everyone with the surrounding environment, and is closely linked to Taoism. Historically, *feng shui* was widely used to orientate buildings, and especially those of a spiritual significance such as tombs. *Feng shui* was suppressed during the Cultural Revolution, but has since then regained popularity.
2. Household registration.
3. Educated youth were sent to the countryside for several reasons. First, high urban unemployment was a major problem. Second, the highly centralized and unified planned economy restricted openings for young people to find employment in cities. Third, as the country began the policy of "agriculture-based, industrial-oriented" economic development, agriculture was in the forefront of the process. So a large number of educated youth were encouraged to go to the countryside to help farmers increase the agricultural production needed for the planned growth. Finally, once the Red Guard movement began in the spring of 1968, it was difficult to control and began to cause chaos nationally. The Red Guards had to be dispersed to ensure the stability of the cities. A report in the People's Daily in December 22, 1968 quoted Mao Zedong as saying, "It is necessary that the educated youth are sent to the countryside to be re-educated by the peasants."
4. Food ration tickets were common in China from 1955 until 1993.
5. The Gang of Four (四人帮) consisted of Chinese Communist Party officials who controlled the main organs of the Communist Party throughout the later stages of the Cultural Revolution. The gang's leading figures were Mao Zedong's last wife Jiang Qing, Zhang Chunqiao, Yao Wenyuan, and Wang Hongwen. It still remains unclear which major decisions were made by Mao Zedong and carried out by the Gang, and which were the result of the Gang of Four's own planning.
6. Hua's (1921–2008) weak personality and loyalty to Maoism did not inspire the Party now weary of the Cultural Revolution, and he quickly came to be seen as having no real ideas of his own. His slogan "Whatever Chairman Mao said, we will say and whatever Chairman Mao did, we will do" was soon sarcastically referred to as "the Two Whatevers" and became a major reason for his fall from power. Deng Xiaoping became the de facto leader of China as his idea for economic reform was adopted by the Party.
7. The pronunciation of a thousand stitches *qian zhen wan xian* (literally "thousand needles ten thousand stitches") sounds like *qian en wan xian* (literally "thousand kindnesses ten thousand appreciations").
8. The formal congratulation ceremony is called *song zhumi* meaning "give congratulations rice".

CHAPTER 4

Shi's Story: Second Daughter

My name is Shi. I'm Zhen and Cheng's second child. I was born in 1955, and my sister Shun is two years older than I am. In the usual Chinese way, I call her Jiejie (older sister) and she calls me meimei (younger sister). My early childhood was, like Shun's, marked by life in the commune and, of course, having to look after brothers and sisters.

Childhood in the Commune

Some of my earliest memories are of hunger. I remember one night Baba came home late from work and Mu cooked him a boiled egg. The noise of cooking drew me from the dark corner of the room where I was trying to sleep to the oil lamp that flickered by the table where Baba was sitting. I stood watching him eat the egg with a little spoon. When he saw me, he gave me a spoonful. It tasted so good. Then I realized that Shun was standing next to me. Even though Baba must have been hungry himself, he gave her a spoonful too. In the flickering light, I saw Baba smile at us, his two little girls. He was always so kind to us.

Like Shun, and later my other brothers and sisters, I was sent to school when I was five years old. I walked to school with Jiejie every morning. Even if there was a big wind or heavy rain, we would not miss school or be late for our classes. My classroom was next to Shun's. Every evening Mu asked us to review what we had studied in class while she was doing mending or some other housework. Mu never had any free time; I always remember her busy doing something. She liked to look at our schoolbooks even though she couldn't read any of the words. Mu had a strong personality and insisted on strict family discipline. None of us children had time to play; all we knew was work, work, and more work.

Even though I was only five, I joined Jiejie and the other villagers working in the commune fields, so I could earn some children's work points. The points may not have been worth a lot, but they all added to our family's rice allocation. It was hard work and very boring, but Jiejie said we had to keep on working even when we were tired, otherwise we wouldn't get the work points for rice. Wherever Jiejie went, I always followed her. Mu told us that when no one was watching we should take some of the sweet potatoes we gathered and hide them in the pockets she had sewn into our coats. I was too frightened to do this because I knew that when the cadres caught anyone stealing they always beat them, so when Jiejie asked me to take one I always cried. She was quick and brave, and often hid a sweet potato in her pocket to take home.

I found school work hard and frequently struggled to finish my homework, but if I got stuck, Shun would always come and help me. She was a good student and received a letter of commendation at the end of each academic year. In all my years at school, I never received such a letter. You see, I wasn't very good at school, and I was behind all the other students in the class. It seemed to me that the more things I didn't understand the more difficulties I faced.

At this time, the entire family's income depended on Baba. He would leave home early in the morning and return after one or two days, sometimes just before the village market. Mu always carefully divided the money Baba earned into two parts; one to buy rice for the family, and the other, chaff for the pigs. There was usually nothing left over. I used to sit with Mu and Baba as they allocated the money. Baba often sighed, "Oh, I am sorry that there is nothing left after everything has been budgeted!" Then he would say, "I will go to work again tomorrow." When the commune distributed rice to each family according to the work points they had earned, I was always happy to collect our family's allocation. In fact Mu was the main one of the family who worked for the commune so we only received very little rice until Baba came home with some money with which he could buy work points to get us more rice from the commune.

In 1961, the collective canteen was closed, and the land was returned to individual families according to the size of the family. All the adults in the village were happy with this, but I didn't really know what it would mean for us. Then Baba and Mu found some land on a distant hillside where they could plant wheat. Although it had a steep gradient, the land seemed to be good for growing crops. As we were scared that the sparrows would eat the wheat, or the crop would be stolen before we could harvest it, we built a small hut in the field and made a scarecrow. Shun and I had to go to the field every day to protect the wheat from the sparrows. Sometimes we didn't want to go, but as Mu was working on another hillside, she could see our field and know if we didn't turn up. I don't know how she could see us from such a long way off, but she did. As soon as the wheat was just ripe, we harvested it to avoid both robbers and sparrows stealing the crop.

Now that we had managed to grow some wheat, Baba thought that it would also be a good idea to raise some chickens for us to eat. He borrowed a hen from a neighbour and bought some fertilized eggs for her to hatch. After a month, the young chicks hatched, and for the following month, we let them run around the yard. Shun and I had to keep our eyes open for eagles because they could easily swoop down and grab one of the chicks. As Grandma Xian also lived with us, she was also on the lookout for the eagles. I remember how every time an eagle attacked a small chicken, Shun, my younger sister, Hua, and me would jump about and shout to try to scare it away. Granma Xian would stand behind us, like a drunk staggering from side-to-side, shouting at the birds. The sound of cackling hens, our shouting, and the screeching of eagles often reverberated around our house. Occasionally, an eagle would manage to catch one of the chicks. When this happened Hua would burst into tears, and Mu would get angry with us. When the chicks were a month old, Baba gave the hen back to her owner with a couple of chicks as a gift.[1] We kept the other chicks so they would grow and provide us with eggs and meat.

Unlike Shun, I didn't pass the enrolment examination to go on to junior high school. I was happy about this because I was then free to do the things I liked. Although I was only 11, I was strong so I did a lot of the work in the fields which we had been allocated. Jiejie and I sometimes had to fetch coal from the nearby town. At first, I thought that it was fun going to the town with her and other girls from our village. I didn't even mind carrying the 15 kg load of coal all the way back home. Then one day, on our way back, Shun lost her balance and slipped into the river. As her head went under the water, I screamed and screamed. Shun managed to get onto her feet and grab hold of a root on the river bank. She kept hold of most of her load, but was unable to climb up the bank with it.

Fortunately, a man heard my screams and ran over and helped Shun to climb out of the water. After that, a kind man at the coal yard arranged for our coal to be loaded on the cart that came to Jin'e, so we no longer needed to make the journey.

Although I was not good at school work, Mu insisted that I should learn a useful skill. She always said, "You need to know some skills that other people can't do otherwise hard days will fill your future." In those days, there were few tailors and their work was in great demand. For a girl, the tailoring skill was also helpful in finding a husband because he knew that you could make some money working at home whilst you looked after the family. So when I was 15, Mu apprenticed me to one of her relatives who was a tailor; my friends thought that I was really lucky to have this opportunity. Baba paid her 10 RMB a month, and she assured them that she could teach me in three months. Ten RMB was a lot of money then, but Baba and Mu were generous. I worked with this lady every day for three months, but always went home to eat. Mu said that in addition to studying hard I should always be eager to help the lady with her housework, which is what I did. Whilst I was apprenticed as a tailor, it meant that I couldn't help Mu so she had to work even harder. Mu kept reminding me of how hard it had been for Baba when he was an apprentice following his master. I did not like Baba's master's family! I remembered all too clearly that one day when I was only three, I followed Baba who was going to work as a chef for a neighbour who was having a special dinner. The sons of his master always wanted to make trouble for him, and on this day, they attacked him and beat him. I ran home to tell Mu so she could get help. Unlike Baba, I had a happy time studying with my master—maybe it was because Baba paid her such a lot of money.

After completing my apprenticeship, one of Baba's friends invited me to work with him for a month to learn how to make dresses. I was always better doing things with my hands than reading books. I began to see the business opportunities that tailoring could offer. My first customer was a childhood friend of Mu. She asked me to make a shirt for her husband. He came to our house so I could take his measurements. I carefully measured his size and arranged the pattern so that I could save a little cloth to make a hanky for her son as a surprise gift. After two days, the shirt was finished. I was very nervous when he came to put on the shirt, but I needn't have been as it fitted perfectly. Her son was also happy to have the little hanky I had made. My customer should have paid me 1 jiao, 1/10th RMB (equivalent to 1 pence in English money), but Mu said we should only charge half this because she was my first customer. After that, wherever she went, she told people what a good tailor I was. Gradually my business began to grow; whenever I managed to save up one RMB, I would buy a length of cloth to enable me to make two shirts. I was really happy that things were going well and I was contributing to the family income. Whenever I visited my old teacher, I would always take her some small gifts to express my thanks to her.

One thing I had wanted to do for a long time was to make shirts for my two younger brothers, Chun and Xia. They had both started school, but had few clothes. Mu had altered the clothes Jiejie and I had worn to fit the boys, but they were baggy and patched. I once saw Xia being laughed at by his classmates because of his poor clothes. I felt sorry for him, but there was nothing I could do at that time. I thought probably the same thing must be happening to Chun, but neither of them complained. To encourage them, I told Chun and Xia that one day I would make each of them a new shirt. Eventually when the time came, they were so happy. I will never forget when they put on the new shirts I had made and they walked proudly along the road. They only wore their shirts at school and at special times like festivals. For many years, I used to make new clothes for them every New Year. By this time there were seven children in our family; Shun was the oldest and Qiu the youngest. I used to work so hard to help Baba and Mu support the family. It's strange—after all I did for the family, how things eventually turned out.

Finding a Marriage Partner

In May 1950, new marriage laws were introduced that required a civil registry for a marriage to be legal, and the marriageable age was raised to 20 for men and 18 for women. Proxy marriage was banned, and both parties had to consent to the marriage. The official slogan was "Men and women are equal; everyone is worth his (or her) salt." Then, in 1980, a revised Marriage Law was adopted that raised the minimum age for marriage to 20 for women and 22 for men.[2] A young couple could now go directly to the registration office taking their Household Registration documents to register their wish to marry. Annual propaganda campaigns were organized all over the country to publicize the new law, which is why I remember it so clearly. Nevertheless, in addition to following the legal registration of marriage, most families also held on to some of the traditional customs like using a matchmaker and arranging a marriage banquet.

As usual, Mu had clear ideas and standards about this. As I was now grown up, matchmakers began visiting us to introduce a man they thought would be suitable for me. If it was somebody Mu didn't like, she directly refused—it was embarrassing! Gradually the matchmaker came to know that Mu was very choosy, and was cautious about suggesting a man for me. I knew that Mu and Shun were concerned to find me a suitable husband and, as I had not been a good student, they wanted to find someone who had some education.

It just so happened that Shun had a colleague who introduced her to a substitute teacher called Hou who was working in a nearby village school. He came from a poor village in the hills and had three sisters and two brothers. Hou was the youngest in his family. I was really nervous when we first met because I didn't know what sort of person he was. I was also worried that his family was poor, but Mu said when you marry, the most important thing is the quality of the man rather than his family. Jiejie said that even though he lived in the hills, he was educated, and as I am skilful, we could make a good life together. Much to my delight, as soon as we met, I liked Hou; indeed, we fell in love. I could hardly believe this as I had known many girls who did not like the man they married. Sometimes they did grow to love their husbands, but on other occasions, their relationship was no more than friendship. I always wanted to have a love marriage, and I was so pleased with the man my parents had chosen for me.

Even though Hou's family was not rich, both our families were concerned to ensure that the marriage followed at least some of the traditions of our area. To tell you the truth, I just wanted to get married. My family insisted that we keep the traditions in case in the future I was bullied by Hou's family then I could leave with my head held high saying that they had asked me to marry him. It was hard for me to believe Hou and I would ever argue or fight, but Baba and Mu insisted on following some of the marriage traditions and so we complied.

Hou's family therefore asked a matchmaker to visit our home to formerly propose the offer of marriage. When my family agreed, Mu went to a fortune-teller to determine what would be an auspicious day for the wedding. Mu, Shun, and my five aunts then went to Hou's family and stayed one night with them. This first step in arranging a marriage is called *kan ren hu* ("look at household"). The seven ladies went to look at the lifestyle of Hou's family and assess their economic standard. When they left the house in the morning, Hou's family prepared gifts for the guests, which included a piece of soap, a face towel, and 2 metres of cloth for each person. After a few days, the matchmaker came again to ask if we wanted to go on to the next step in the marriage. We all agreed to this.

The second step is *zou dong xi* ("walking gift"). My family chose three days, one in each of the next three months, for Hou's family to visit our family. On each visit, they brought 1 kg of white sugar, 1 kg of rock sugar, two pieces of the best pork each weighing about 1.5 kg, and two bottles of wine. The third step is called *dai hua* ("wear flower"). This time Hou's family gave 8 metres of cloth, two pig legs, four bottles of wine, 2 kg of white sugar, 2 kg of rock sugar, 2 kg of mixed candy, and 2 kg of green tea. After my family had received these gifts, Hou's family sent a letter written on red paper with the Chinese character *yun* (允) meaning "allowed". The fourth step was *kai geng* ("opening birthday") which commenced with my family sending my date of birth to Hou's family. Hou's family then hired a fortune-teller to find an auspicious day based on the dates of birth of Hou and me. The matchmaker then sent the date to us. My family asked another fortune-teller to check whether the date was right, and as both fortune-tellers agreed that the date was auspicious, the matter was fixed.

The fifth and final stage was the day of our marriage. My family gave Hou's family some gifts, which consisted of a chair, a table, a wardrobe, and a wooden barrel to wash one's feet in before going to bed. Hou's family killed a pig, decorated their house, and prepared the bedroom for us. Then on the agreed date my uncle, aunt, sister, and eldest brother went with me to spend the night at Hou's family home: by tradition, my parents are not allowed to go. After staying the night, they returned home. Usually this whole procedure could take as long as two years, but in my case, it took three years because Mu wanted me to stay at home for another year to help with the younger children.

In 1981, I finally left to live with Hou and his family in Guangming. Before leaving Jin'e, my family held a big farewell party for me, and I received many gifts from the neighbours since my family had built up good relationships with them over the past years. I was given towels, cloth, and perfumed soap. Jiejie had a sewing machine coupon from her friend and as a dowry gift bought me a new sewing machine—a very expensive present at that time—with her salary.[3]

When I left home, Baba told me to respect my parents-in-law and to do my best to support Hou. As I was leaving I turned back to look at Mu, and I saw she had tears in her eyes. I left six younger brothers and sisters of whom the youngest was only six. Ever since Shun had gone to college in

1971, I had tried my best to support the family and help raise my younger brothers and sisters. Because Baba often worked away from home, I knew how hard Mu had to work for the family. Our years of working together had built a deep bond between us. I knew she was sad. From that day on, I would never work hard again for the family of my birth because I now had joined a new family and I must care for them. Once I left my old home as a married daughter, I knew that from now on I would only be a guest in that house. There was no room there for me anymore. Baba, Mu, and all my brothers and sisters would soon be distant from my daily life. Although I was looking forward to my marriage with Hou, I wished I could stay in my old home forever. I promised Mu, and Jiejie too, that I would often come back to visit them and would always be willing to help support the family.

Shun was still responsible for the family, and after reflecting on the time, effort and cost of my wedding, she made a sensible decision. She argued that a traditional marriage was not a good practice to follow when the younger children got married. We had spent a lot of money, and had many towels and perfumed soaps left over. Since there were many brothers and sisters, the wedding arrangements had to be simpler and cheaper. Baba did not agree, but Shun took charge and had her way. She was the eldest daughter, had education, and a stable government job, so Baba kept quiet. Overall, I think that Shun was right in her views. I would have been just as happy to have had a simple wedding; I only did what the family said should be done. I was 23 when I first met Hou; I did not live with him until I was 26.

Marriage to Hou was not as wonderful as I had first hoped. I went to live in his home with his family in Guangming, and although we had a small room to ourselves, the family was ever present. As the house was small and we all lived under the same roof, Hou and I had little space for ourselves. I was also upset that Hou had a closer relationship with his father than with me. I consider myself a hard worker, but to provide for the family both Hou and I had to work hard. Usually a new wife would, for the first few months after marriage, only work in the house, because if she worked outside neighbours would make jokes about sex to embarrass her. But after only two weeks, I had to go and work in the fields and try to ignore the rude comments made by the neighbours. Not only did I work the fields and cook the food, I also tried to make some money by tailoring. So, you can see that by the end of the day Hou and I were often very tired. People say that I have a strong personality like my mother, which is probably true. I loved Hou, but even so, we often had disagreements and argued.

As we were living in the same house as Hou's three sisters you might expect them to work hard for the family, but they were often lazy. When I talked to the other women in Guangming, they said that they knew this and were sorry for me. Hou sometimes got annoyed with me and accused me of gossiping about his family in the market, whereas in actual fact it was other people who were telling me what they knew of his sisters. Don't you think that he should have supported me, and not accused me of gossiping? Husband and wife are now equal, so why should I be the submissive young bride like in old times? During the first year of our married life, Hou would often go to Shun to ask her to help us resolve our disputes.

New Business Opportunities

Although Hou had a job as a primary school teacher, his wage was very small. He left for school around 7 a.m. when it was still dark in winter. At school, he was a maths teacher and taught the sixth grade students. He would come back home around 3 p.m. to have lunch. Sometimes he needed to visit parents of the students, and would not come back home until late in the evening. You can see that we didn't have much time together, and also Hou was not talkative like me. He liked to consider things deeply before making any decision.

It's true that Hou was well respected in the village—he was educated and could write Chinese characters well. For example, when there was a wedding or a funeral in the village the host would invite relatives, friends, and neighbours to join the occasion. It was the custom that the guests would bring gifts, and so the host would ask a couple of men to sit at the entrance to receive the gifts and make a record in a ledger of who gave what gift. Then, when one of the guests held a celebration, the family would reciprocate by giving a gift of a similar value, or even little more. At these occasions, Hou was always asked to make the record because his writing was so clear and easy to read.

Like Hou, I had to work hard to provide for the family. Every two or three days, I would walk to Jin'e town market, which was a two-hour walk. I tried to arrive about 9 a.m. and leave the market at 2 p.m. so I could get home at 4 p.m. I liked going back to Jin'e as there were many people there who I had known for many years, and we could have a good chat whilst doing business. Although the economy was improving, the villagers still only had a little spare money, so if they wanted a new coat or pair of trousers, they would buy the cloth and ask a tailor to make what they wanted. I set up my sewing machine next to Ze's cloth stall. After the customers bought cloth from Ze, they would ask me to make it into the clothes they wanted. I then measured the customers, making a careful record. At the end of the day, I would load the cloth into my backpack and carry the load the two-hour journey back home where I would make the clothes they had ordered. I left my sewing machine with Ze who, on the days when there was no market, kept his stock of cloth at Qi's home.

In the second year of our marriage, I gave birth to a lovely baby girl, but the birth of a girl was a disappointment to Hou's family as they wanted a boy. My family in turn were disappointed with Hou who they said was a person with very fixed ideas and refused to compromise. So, when the time came for the first-month's rite for the baby, Baba and Mu did not come to celebrate. I used to carry the little girl around with me strapped on my back, so that I could still do my tailoring and some housework. Sometime my mother-in-law would give me a hand, but not often.

When Fu was six months old, we separated from Hou's family. Although we continued to live under the same roof, Hou, Fu, and I no longer cooked and ate our meals with Hou's family. We now had our own bedroom, a dining room, two small pigs, and three fields. I can't tell you how happy I was with this because it meant that I could now make some money and work for my own family.

A couple of years later I gave birth to a second child—a boy. Because the one-child policy was now in effect we had to pay a fine for breaking the policy, but it was much smaller than the fine Shun and Ze had to pay for their second child. This was because Shun was a professional teacher paid by the government and so was expected to follow government policy. My father-in-law was a nice man. He saw how hard it was for me to look after the children so he made a big cradle for the little boy. By this time, Fu was three years old and I could sometimes play with them when I was working at home. I could never imagine how Mu had raised eight children. However, when I went to the market in town my parents-in-law did help to look after the children.

In 1987, Hou was granted a scholarship to attend teacher training college; the very same college that Shun had attended some years before. When he told me about this, he hesitated as to whether he should go or not as he knew this would mean extra work for me. However, I was very pleased because I knew that once he finished college he would get official teacher status like Shun. I supported him but he was right, the following two years were tough for me. I had to take care of the children and work in the fields. At the time there was no telephone so if I ever had to contact him in an emergency, I had to send him a telegram from the post office in town. I usually received a reply in a couple of days. I always liked the sound of Di-Di-Da-Da of the telegraph machine because it sounded as if I was talking with Hou. Although I had previously argued with Hou's sisters because they didn't work hard, when Hou was away I kept quiet. I really disliked lazy people.

Harvest time is one of the busiest times in the whole calendar year for farmers, as the crops have to be gathered at the critical time. Villagers help each other by giving their labour free so it was very important to have a good relationship with your neighbours and to treat them well by giving them food and drink. Otherwise, they would give you any old excuse as to why they couldn't help you. As neither Hou nor I could return the labour, I always tried to ensure that I gave the best food I could to those who came to help us.

When Hou finally returned from college in 1989, he was promoted to Head Teacher, which meant that we could move into accommodation at the school set aside for the head teacher. It was so good to have more rooms in our home. About this time, Hou's three sisters married local famers. Hou and his older brother paid a monthly contribution to support his parents who continued to do some farming and raise pigs. In the busy farming season, we would all come together to help plant their fields or harvest for them.

There were about 2000 people living in Guangming, and they were organized into seven production teams. These teams were a continuation from the time of the commune system. The village had three leadership positions: the village head, the secretary of the Communist Party, and the clerical assistant. These people needed to be upright and impartial, and were usually members of one of the larger clans. If a family had any troubles, they would initially turn for help to one of these three officials. As Hou had a pleasant personality, was one of the most educated people in the village, and came from one of the largest clans, the villagers wanted him to be one of the village leaders. Of course, he accepted the role, but just as I feared, he was busier than ever.

For some time I had been thinking about setting up a shop in the village, but I had little influence with the previous village leaders. Once Hou was appointed as one of the village heads, I was able to put my plan into operation. I opened a stall next to the school and started selling household goods, fertilizer, and other items. The villagers really liked this as it saved them having to make the trip to town and carry things back. As I had to pay for transporting the goods to our village, I had to charge a bit more than the town shops. Nevertheless, my shop quickly became a centre where people would meet and chat. After a while, I installed a telephone in our house and this soon became the way villagers could contact their relatives working as migrant labourers in different cities. I could also contact my suppliers. Sure, I charged a fee—but a fair one—for the minutes they used; it made some money for us. Hou sometimes accused me of taking advantage of his position. It is difficult to understand why he thought like this but he failed to see how the country was changing. This was a business opportunity enabling me to provide a good service for the village. He should have been thanking rather than criticizing me.

Sometimes mother-in-law would come to stay with us for several days. I didn't mind this too much until I found that, without asking me, she was taking things from the store to give to her daughters. If she had asked, I would have given the things to her, but she never did. She kept on taking things and this really annoyed me. When I told her to stop, she argued with me saying that she was free to do what she wanted in her son's home. Hou took her side and also argued with me. Neither of them understood how to do business, and that I needed to account for the losses.

One traditional festival in the village was Qingming; during this week, all the students from the township would come to visit a special tomb near our school.[4] The tomb was of a martyr who was killed in the village fighting for the Communists against the Kuomintang.[5] Every year, the counsellor of the Young Pioneers would tell the story of the martyr's heroic death. Students from each school would place a wreath of flowers on his tomb, while all the other students would stand in silent tribute. For me, it was a very busy week because many students would visit the school, and they would all want to buy snacks. Shun and her child would also come and visit, and they would have dinner with us.

As the school was located in the village centre and there were no other stores, business was brisk and quickly expanded. By 1994, I was the wealthiest of Zhen's eight children, and for the next four years, I was the main source of income for Zhen's family as well as my own. Like my elder sister Shun, I cared about my family and was willing to support them even though Hou didn't like me giving them money. I told Hou that as it was me who was making the money, I had the right to use my money in any way I wished.

Let me tell you about some of the things I did for the family. I paid for my youngest brother Dong to study at high school, an opportunity I never had myself. Then, I helped pay for the trouble that my third brother Qiu created for the family. Although by this time he was not at home, the Wang family continued to cause Zhen's family trouble. They often hired people to sit in front of Zhen's home to fight any family members who came there. Shun decided to take the matter to court, but to win the case she needed a lawyer. All this needed money. Who do you think paid the lawyer's fees required to stop the blockage? It was not cheap I can tell you! After the argument with my eldest brother, I stopped supporting the family, but continued to give money to Zhen every month until 2013.

New Conflicts

In 2004, after Hou had been the headmaster of the village school for ten years, Hou and I and the two children moved to Jin'e. I had managed to buy a plot of land in the town centre, and that's where we built a beautiful house. The house was located in the new development area of Jin'e along the only street going to the county centre. I expanded my business to include selling cement and fertilizer. In our area, it is the custom when you move into a new house to hold a party to which family and friends are invited. At such an event guests give money to the hosts, each sum being carefully noted in a ledger as a family record. When Hou and I moved into our new house none of my family came, so they didn't contribute any money. To hide my shame, I gave some of my own money to the person making the record of gifts and told them it came from Shun and other family members. In this way, I tried to keep face and help improve Hou's opinion of my family.

Even though Hou and I were now living in Jin'e, the villagers from Guangming would still come to our home to ask his advice on village matters. They often came into our nice new house with their muddy shoes and clothes. Wouldn't that make you angry? I told them to get out as they were making the house dirty. Hou, rather than supporting me, said that as they are from his village I should recognize that they were poor and needed his help.

At this time, my eldest brother Chun worked in the town veterinary station. The station built a new office right next to my own house. At first, it seemed good to have my family so near, but problems soon arose. A piece of land that was part of the veterinary station wasn't being used; I thought of a good way to make use of it. I asked Chun as the principal of the veterinarian station to let me use the land. But, do you know what? Chun objected! Can you imagine that? After all I had done for the family in the past, don't you think that he could give me some small advantage? However, he stood on his principles! I told him that other officials in the country do this sort of thing for their family. But, he would not budge!

Not long after that, another conflict arose in the family. In 2005, my younger brother Xia became my business partner. I expanded my house adding two floors each of 300 square metres. I used the first floor as a store for our stock, on the second was an apartment where we lived. For three years, the arrangement worked well, but in the fourth year a problem arose. Our business was selling farming products including different types of fertilizers. The business had expanded to cover the whole of the county, so Xia moved to the county town. He became responsible for some of the government-assisted programmes to help poorer peasants. One day, Xia's assistant asked me to approve some procedures he said were required by a government programme. I refused saying that it was both unnecessary and too much trouble. Xia disagreed with me and said that I had to implement the programme policy, and the two of us had a big argument right there in the store. The assistant quickly called Shun who came over to help, but she could not find a way to resolve our dispute.

From that time on, Hou kept his distance from Zhen's family, and didn't want me to be in contact with my brothers as they always seemed to cause trouble. The following year, Hou and I fought again and I shouted out loudly. Zhen, Shun, and Chun heard us fighting because, as I said before, they were living in the house next door. They were worried that Hou would hurt me, so they came to our door. Hou was annoyed at their interference so he marched out of the house. When our son got home, he went out to look for his father. He also went to Shun's family and told them that they should not interfere with his parent's life. Since then my family has remained estranged from Zhen's family. Even though we still live next door, to this day we never speak to each other.

Time has passed and things have changed little. Mu is in good health and lives with Chun next door. I often see her pass my house on her way to visit my third sister, or to go the temple. Occasionally, I call out hello to her. I would really like to invite her to come in and sit in my big house, but I know Hou would not be happy with this. Mu doesn't like Hou because she can't forget that he hit me. Whenever Mu passes by my heart calls out to her, and I believe in her heart she responds, "My sweet, how is everything going? Do take care yourself and don't work too hard." I believe there is always a place in her heart that belongs to me.

NOTES

1. The number had to be an even number as this signifies good luck.
2. Population Council (1981). "China's New Marriage Law" *Population and Development Review*, 7(2), 369–372.
3. A dowry is articles or money brought by a bride to her husband on their marriage. At this time, many items were rationed and could only he bought if you had a coupon as well as the money. A village would only be allowed one sewing machine coupon a year, and so this coupon was especially prized.
4. The Qingming Festival, also known as "Tomb-Sweeping Day" in English, is a traditional Chinese festival held on the first day of the fifth solar term of the traditional Chinese lunar calendar. On this day, tombs are swept and ancestors are venerated with offerings of food and the burning of joss paper.
5. The Kuomintang (KMT) was the Nationalist Party of China founded by Song Jiaoren and Sun Yat-sen shortly after the Xinhai Revolution of 1911. Sun Yat-sen was the provisional president, but he did not have military power and ceded the presidency to the military leader Yuan Shikai. After Yuan's death, China broke up into areas ruled by warlords, and the KMT was only able to control the south of the country. Later under the leadership of Chiang Kai-shek, the KMT formed the National Revolutionary Army and succeeded in unifying most of China in 1928. The KMT ruled mainland China from 1928 until it was defeated by the CCP during the Chinese Civil War.

CHAPTER 5

Hua's Story: Third Daughter

There is an old Chinese proverb which says, "Land is life blood. Without it brothers cannot live." The family and the land have always been important to the peasants. I should have remembered that. I sold our land and insulted my family. Years later, I still feel ashamed of all that happened, but I am grateful that Mu has accepted my husband and me back in the family.

In 2002, a formal ceremony of apology took place in the best restaurant in town. Mu sat in the place of honour in the middle of the tables, the other members sat in accordance with their age and rank. My husband Guang and I went individually to each of them and said we wanted to apologize for our past actions towards Baba and Mu and we invited them to witness the ceremony. Guang and I knelt in front of Mu and formally apologized for what we had done; we expressed the guilt we felt and asked to be received back into the family. I can't describe to you the shame we both felt as we knelt there with everyone watching. Mu sat with her rugged face showing no emotion, but I knew her eyes were bright as she watched. After I spoke, I looked and saw tears running down her face, and she quietly said, "Don't go away again. If Baba were here he would forgive you." Then she drew me close and hugged me. Oh, the relief! I was so pleased to feel Mu once again holding me with her big strong hands. I promised, "I will stay with you forever." Even though I have my own home with my husband and daughter, in my heart I still think of the little house where I grew up with Baba and Mu as being my real home.

While Mu has forgiven us and was happy to receive us back, we knew that some other family members still feel hurt by what we did. I do hope that all of us, her children, can remain in a loving relationship with Mu and remember that we are brothers and sisters. Guang and I will try to make amends for what we did.

* * *

I was born in 1957, Zhen and Cheng's third child. Like my elder sisters, Shun and Shi, I grew up in the commune. Some of my earliest memories are of Shun going off to school wrapped in her coat to protect her from the cold. In time, I went to the same school, but by then there was more food. I remember little of the famine only that when Mu and Baba spoke about it, it was with sorrow. I remember looking after my younger brother, Chun. He was the first son in the family and our parents were so happy at his birth two years after me. When Shun and Shi helped Mu farm, Grandma Xian and I stayed at home with Chun. Chun was cute and obedient. Even though he was the first son, he had to follow the same strict rules as us, his sisters. Baba and Mu never spoilt him! I remember that Shun and Shi were always reading school books, and at the beginning of the academic year, they would give their old books to me. Mu would ask me to read the books even before classes started. Mu seemed obsessed with books and wanted to listen to me reading every day. Even though the famine was over, we were still poor and as Shun and Shi grew bigger their old clothes that Mu had altered were passed on to me.

From 1961, the government allowed village markets to be held once again, and farmers were able to cultivate fields for their own use. The produce they grew they could eat themselves and any extra they were free to sell at the market. Our fields always did well. We planted corn, sweet potato, sorghum, peas, and other crops like Chinese cabbage and radish. Mu said that everything we planted should be a potential main course of a meal. At the Spring Festival, we would kill one of the pigs. This pig was the only meat we would have for the whole year, and so we carefully used it in various dishes. I liked the taste of the meat! Baba was good at many things, and to ensure that we would have a good New Year's celebration, he grew a wide range of crops and also made a variety of sweets for us children. Money was always in short supply, and unlike children today, we were never given pocket money.

One day in 1966, when I was in the third grade of primary school, our teacher told us we didn't need to come to school any more since it would be closed as part of what the teacher called the *Dachuanlian*, revolutionary tours around the country. We were also told that some of the middle school students would go to Beijing, which was far away from where we lived. I didn't really understand what it was all about, but some of the older children seemed to be excited about it. Shun and Shi also did not go to school, but none of us were simply allowed to play as there were many things to do at home. Every day, Shun and Shi went to work for the commune with Mu. As Baba was a vet, he needed to travel out to different villages to help the farmers with their animals. This meant that Grandma Xian and I stayed at home to look after my two young brothers, Chun and Xia. Looking after the boys was really troublesome as they were naughty and I had a lot of housework to do. Every morning Mu, Shun, and Shi left home around 7:30 a.m. with a hoe or some other tool to walk to one of the commune fields that could be as much as a couple of kilometres away. In the late afternoon, they returned tired after hours of hard work. After eight months, the school re-opened and I was so happy to go back to my lessons.

Throughout the whole year, I rarely saw my parents smile as they had to keep working and only had a few hours of sleep at night. They only seemed to smile at the Spring Festival even though they still felt exhausted from all their work. We have a belief that at New Year, the kitchen god goes back to heaven for a few days to report on our situation to the great god. If the family lived in harmony, it meant blessing for the coming year, but if we quarrelled, we would be punished. Even if we did something wrong near the Spring Festival, Baba and Mu were neither angry with us nor beat us, so we were free to play happily without being punished. On the eve of the Spring Festival, we would sit at the table, laughing and chatting ready to enjoy a sumptuous feast.

After graduating from primary school, I succeeded in gaining admission to junior high school; the same school that Shun had attended, but my scores were never as good as hers. Nevertheless, in my third year the teacher told me I was being recommended to study at senior high school. I think this was because my family had a peasant background and my academic score had met the basic requirements. This news made me very happy, but I wasn't sure if my parents would support me. I talked this over with Baba and Mu. Baba was quiet; he had a quiet personality, but I knew he loved me as he did all his children. Mu said "to study more is always good" and, turning to Baba, asked if there was any extra money to support me. I knew that if I stayed at school for two more years, this would not only cost the family extra money, but would also mean one less worker. Some of our neighbours thought this was a silly thing to do because at the time universities were closed. The family discussed the options with Shun, and after a few days, they decided to support me through senior school. Without their support, I too might have had to go back to work in the fields.

At senior high school, I found studying much harder than I had expected and even though I tried my best, my scores was only in the middle of the bottom half of the class. I was disappointed by my low scores. After the two years, just as our neighbours had predicted, the universities had not reopened, and I had nowhere to go other than back home to work with the family.

I still remember one night in 1977, as we were preparing dinner, we turned on the radio to listen to the eight o'clock news. The China national radio ran an announcement that the State Council and the Ministry of Education would soon recommence the National College Entrance Examination, which we call "the *gaokao*". I was both shocked and delighted at the same time. I could hardly believe that this was real. The *gaokao* was what I wanted to take before leaving senior high school. All across the country, many young people cheered and even wept as the news spread. The *gaokao* soon became a hot topic of discussion even in our little town. It meant that the destinies of students would change. Those who had been sent to the countryside could return to their home cities and their previous work. It was also a sign of our country's emerging future.

I immediately started preparing for the examination, but quickly faced many difficulties. First, since I had to work in the fields for the commune I could only study at night. Second, with no bookshop in our area I couldn't find any revision materials. I had some books from my school years, but the contents of many were political such as the *Quotations from Chairman Mao*. Third, without electric lighting I could only read by the light of the kerosene lamp. Everything was still scarce, even writing paper. As it was winter and so cold, I could only get warm by stamping my feet and rubbing my hands. It was really difficult to concentrate. Without a tutor to help me, I struggled even to understand the questions.

As the *gaokao* had been interrupted for ten years, the age of the people who came to the examination was wide ranging from 16 to 40. You could even find both parents and their children sitting the examination at the same time. It was held over two days, and the subjects were mathematics, Chinese, English, politics, physics, and chemistry. I can still remember some of the questions. One in the politics paper asked, "Who was the author of Internationale song?" The English exam asked us to translate: "I'm taking the National College Entrance Examination and I hope to go to study at university. I will strive to study hard and become a 'Red' and professional expert."[1] In the Chinese paper we were asked to analyse the structure of the sentence: "In order to achieve the great ideal of Communism, I will contribute my whole life and time." As you can guess, the examination was very competitive and only 2% of those who sat it finally went to university. I was not among this elite few, but I did have the chance to stay on at school for another year. The next year, to the disappointment of my whole family, I again failed the examination.

Even though Shun was married, she continued to return home every three or four days because as the eldest child she felt responsible for the younger children. Then one day she arrived with great excitement. She told me that a village school was looking for a substitute teacher, and she had recommended me to the head teacher. At that time, working as a substitute teacher was a good job even though the salary was small. I was really happy about this but wondered how I could teach without any professional training. Shun had already thought about this. She sat me down and spent an hour telling me about her own experiences. Then she got a textbook from my younger brother Qiu and showed me how she would teach that subject. After my brothers and sister had arrived back from school and we had eaten dinner, Shun asked them all to sit in the living room whilst I taught them with the method she had taught me. People were a resource my family always had! But I was so embarrassed standing there in front of my brothers and sister that I froze and couldn't say a word. Shun came and stood beside me and told me what to say. I repeated each sentence, and after half-an-hour, I felt more confident. On the next day, I went to Shun's class to see how she taught and I interacted with her students. After four days, although I was still nervous, I started my teaching job.

Far way in Anhui Province, something quite remarkable happened in 1979 that was going to affect all of us.[2] In a village there, 18 households signed a contract with the cadres in which the village land was distributed to each family to grow their own crops. The cadres did not report this to their leaders, and everyone waited to see if they would be punished by the government for dereliction of duty. The farmers agreed that if anything bad happened to the cadres they would look after their families. When harvest time came, the crop production was much greater than in previous years. Somebody mentioned this to Deng Xiaoping who was then the President of China. He praised the village saying that what they had done should be adopted nationwide. At the beginning of the 1980s, we heard that the commune in our village was to be closed and the land given to farmers according to the "Household Contract Responsibility System". My family was excited about this because as we had many children, we would have a big allocation of land. When the commune finally closed, a village committee was established and land distributed to each family in terms of its size. Shun did not get land because she had a city residence permit—*hukou*. Shi got land in the village where she lived after her marriage. Nevertheless, our family got land for eight people. What was even more exciting was that most of the land we had been allocated was close to the town centre. Under the Household Contract Responsibility System, the land continued to be owned by the nation, but the farmers had the right to use the land. This differed from the Land Reform of 1950 which gave the farmer ownership of the land. Baba said that maybe in the future, we could build a house in the town centre. At the time, I thought that this was an impossible dream, and Baba was merely joking.

In the following months, we all worked hard on our fields. Some mornings before my brothers and sister went to school, they also worked with Mu in the fields. In the afternoon, when school finished, they went back to the fields. When Baba returned from his veterinarian work, he spent all his spare time farming. That year some of our neighbours managed to grow more food than they needed to eat, and were able to sell the surplus in the market. We grew enough for our own family, and we raised ten chickens and a few more pigs. At the end of the year, we killed a big pig and two chickens for our Spring Festival feast. We were all so happy! In the following year, Baba bought a mother pig and five chicks.

Even during happy periods, sad things happen. Grandma Xian died. She always got up early to have breakfast with us before the boys went to school. One morning, she did not appear for breakfast, so Qiu went to call her. There was no response. Baba went to her bed and touched her, only to find her body was cold. We cried because we all loved her. During the famine, Mu had occasionally complained that she was an extra mouth to feed because her bound feet meant that she could not work. However, when Baba and Mu were working outside, it was Grandma Xian who stayed with us and told us stories about her life. She had had two sons, but gave the younger one away because she did not have enough food to feed both children. Sadly she said, "That's life!" I remember too her saying that maybe her son still blamed her for abandoning him and perhaps he still hated her, but it was more important that he lived. Because Grandma stayed with us, we were not afraid even if Mu and Baba did not return home until late in the evenings. Grandma was soft and gentle, and whenever Mu punished us, Grandma would always comfort us by holding us close to her thin warm body. We were all very sad when she died, but Baba said that it was a blessing that she died peacefully without any illness. Baba built a tomb for her on the hill next to his step-father.

Soon the local market reopened, and some young men from Wenxing town set up their own stalls. One of these young men was Guang. He came to our town every other day to sell some commodities, which he had bought in the city. He was tall with beautiful eyes. I sometimes went to his stall to buy salt and washing powder. In 1981, when I was 24, Guang and I told the family that we wanted to get married. In the same year, Shi was going to marry and our family was preparing a dowry for her. My oldest brother, Chun was 20 and Dong, the youngest one, only 6; all the other children were still at school. Shun and Mu hoped I would stay at home to help support the family for a couple more years until Chun started work. I persisted that I wanted to marry Guang soon. I am not like Shi, always considering the family. I wanted to have my own life and start my own family. Shun warned me that if I married Guang immediately the family wouldn't be able to give either gifts or arrange a formal celebration for me. Since the family had already arranged the celebrations for Shi, they could not afford to arrange another one for me. If we held two celebrations in the same year, our friends would have to prepare two gifts and we would have to hold two feasts. This would be a problem for both our friends and my family. I understood all this but I didn't think it was important. I told Shun this. Guang and I loved each other, so we went to the government office to register our marriage.

After we married, I left my job at the village school. Guang and I rented a house in Jin'e where we continued his business, which became very busy. We soon started making good money and wanted to expand. Guang had studied some medicine when he was in the army, and although he was not a qualified doctor he was able to make up prescriptions. We thought that if we could invite a retired doctor to join us and provide him a place to sit and write prescriptions, he could charge the patient a fee, and we could sell the medicines. What we needed was our own house where we could live and open our medicine shop, and for this, we needed a plot of land on which to build.

After I married, I sometimes visited Baba and Mu, but not regularly like Shun. Shun had two children who had a close relationship with their grandparents, and they liked to stay with their young uncles. Although Guang and I had by then been married for several years, we had no children. We both wanted children, but never succeeded. I had therefore given all my energies to our business, which was making us a good profit. We decided to approach the family to ask if they would give us a plot of land on which we could build a house. The family discussed the suggestion, and Baba said that as he had not given me any gift when I married, the family should give us a portion of land. It was therefore agreed to divide the land near the town centre into four parts. Guang and I would get one plot which would be bigger than my share of the inheritance.

In order to build a house on the land we needed to get a permit from the local authority. As part of the agreement, the family asked us to arrange the legal entitlement documents from the authority, not only for our own house but for all four plots. I promised to do this and to pay the 40 RMB needed for the family to register the necessary documents. I agreed even though I was reluctant to pay this big amount of money.

In the following year, both Zhen's family and Guang and I started building our houses on adjoining plots at the side of the road near the town centre. During the construction process, one of the local cadres came to check our documentation. Shun asked me to show her the document; to her horror she found that the document was only for my house, nothing else. As I had failed to register the other plots, the construction of Zhen's house had to stop immediately. At the time, it was difficult to reapply for building permission and it meant considerable additional paperwork, time, and cost. Construction on Zhen's house was delayed for a year, while I was able to continue building my house. Although the family was annoyed that I had not done what had been asked of me, they were still willing to help with some of the work on our house. Several of them helped with various practical jobs; my young brothers, for example, slept in the construction site to prevent anybody stealing the materials. Then, something else happened that angered the whole family.

A friend of mine also wanted to build a house, so I asked Shun whether she could have the remaining plot. Shun refused saying that all three were needed for the family. As my friend was really nice to me and we always helped each other, I told her not to worry because I would go directly to

Baba for his permission. I thought that as the family had so much land in the town centre it wouldn't be a problem if we let my friend have some. I remembered that it would soon be Baba's birthday, so I invited him for dinner at my new house and I also invited my friend to join us. During the dinner, my friend and I tried to put Baba in a good mood, and he got drunk. When he learned that my friend wanted to buy one of our plots of land, he was quite happy to give his permission with a cheap price. He then and there signed a document giving her a plot, and because there was no previous legal document, it meant that this document was valid. Of the four plots of land the family owned, I had one, my friend had one, and Zhen's family had two, on one of which they were building a house.

On the following day, when Shun heard about this she was so angry. She shouted at Baba and reminded him of the saying, "Land is life blood. Without it brothers cannot live." Baba was so distraught at the foolish thing that he had done that he straightaway came to my house asking if he could take back the document. However, my friend had first thing that morning submitted the document to the government office. Shun was furious with me and shouted at me. "You are a disappointment to us and do not deserve all the help the family has given you over all those years." Shun was worried that our four brothers would not have enough land on which to build their houses and get married. The whole family was angry with me at what I had done, and immediately broke off all communication with me.

Guang and I moved into our new house. As we had planned, we set up our business on the ground floor of the house. We not only sold medicines, but daily necessities like soap and spirit. In 1992, Deng Xiaoping made his famous Southern Inspection Speech in Shenzhen after which China fully implemented a market economy and many people started expanding their businesses. We expanded our business even more rapidly and made good money. During the 1990s, Zhen's family faced major financial and social difficulties. Chun and Xia were both at college, my younger sister Kai and my two youngest brothers, Qiu and Dong, were still at school. When Qiu had a conflict with a boy at school, he had to leave the village. I am sorry to say that unlike Shun and Shi, I did not give any help to the family. Even when my parents passed by my house, I ignored them and did not invite them to come in.

In 1996, my neighbour told me Baba was very ill, and that Chun was trying his best to pay for Baba's treatment. I felt guilty about what I had done to Baba, and I wanted to see him before he died. I therefore decided to talk to my uncle Qi, Zhen's brother. He agreed to pass on my wish to Chun. Qi told me later that Chun said that Baba should decide whether he wanted to see me or not. Baba agreed to meet me. I still remember how much I regretted what I had done. I could only hold his hand and say, "I'm sorry." He looked at me with sad eyes. I knew I was still his little girl and he forgave me.

Baba died in 1997. His death was announced by fire crackers, awakening the neighbourhood early in the morning. As my house was right next door to that of his sons, I could see the rest of the family busy making the funeral arrangements. At such a time, all the blood relatives of the deceased were expected to dress in white clothes with long sleeves and to cry during the festival. When I knelt at the coffin with my brothers, I realized that all of them had now grown up and were strong enough. Chun was the head of the vet station, Xia had a business in the city, and Dong was a head teacher of a nice primary school. When I saw how close they were to Shun and Shi, I realized how great the gap was between them and me.

Baba's funeral was held in the house next to ours. The walls were covered in white paper as a sign of mourning, and a cloth was draped over the doorway. Baba's body was washed and dressed in new clothes of dark blue before being placed in the coffin; his face was covered with a yellow cloth. The coffin was placed in the living room; a portrait of Baba was hung on the wall. Small gifts of food were then placed near the body. As was the local custom, a member of the family stayed with the body until the date set by the diviner as being most auspicious for the entombment. The correct performance of all the arrangements was then overseen by a Taoist priest.

On the auspicious day, the coffin was carried to the tomb, again with the sound of fire crackers. Strong men carried the coffin, with the head of the corpse always pointed forward. Family members followed behind dressed in white, and holding onto a white cloth trailing back from the coffin. It took nearly two hours for the body to be carried to the site of the tomb as we made occasional stops. Baba had chosen the site himself because he thought that it was a good place for *feng shui*. The family had built a rectangular tomb on the site and set a stone slab at the front. On it a local calligrapher had carved Cheng's name, and the names of his sons and daughters. During the seven days following a death, it was believed that the dead person's soul would try to return to the family home. So, at night a red sign was placed outside the house saying who it belonged to, and all other lights were extinguished. The family inside kept very quiet so as not to scare the soul away and it got lost.

In our town, it is the custom for the family to invite a Taoist priest to perform various religious rituals on the following three Chinese New Year days: the first day of the first year, the second day of the second year and the third day of the third year. In the first year, many relatives came to Chun's house to remember Baba. As the family had disapproved of my behaviour, I tried to keep out of sight as Guang and I didn't know what to do. Then, we heard that a relative of Guang had died and his son was holding the same rituals for him. We decided to go to stay with Guang's relative, so we closed the shop and left. By doing this, we once again hurt Zhen and my brothers.

In 2002, the government brought in changes to its healthcare policy which required that all medicines had to be sold under the direction of a registered doctor, and each village was to have a qualified doctor. The village doctor was responsible for the village medical store which stocked medicines covered by social insurance. For some common complaints like flu and headaches, the villagers didn't need to pay for the medicine. Although this greatly improved the peasants' overall healthcare, it meant that our business was finished. We lost many of our customers and were left with only empty glass cabinets in which we used to store our medicines. That same year, at 45 years of age, I found I was pregnant. This was one joy amongst our many problems. Guang and I were delighted, and I gave birth to a lovely little girl.

Then in the midst of all this, another serious problem occurred: one of our former patients took out a lawsuit against Guang. Guang had never before faced such a situation and had no idea of how to deal with the matter. Guang and I realized that we desperately needed the help of Dong, my fourth brother who was a cadre and knew how to deal with such situations. So after a division of 15 years, we turned to the family for help. We first went to talk to Mu about our trouble as we knew she still cared for us. She told us we should go to talk with Dong but she didn't know if he would support us.

With fear and shame, we went to see Dong. We told him what happened, but he just sat there stony-faced and said nothing. We left! Afterwards we talked to Mu again, but she only said she would accept whatever Dong decided. Later we heard that Dong had discussed the matter with his brothers. The family finally decided that if we held a formal ceremony of repentance towards Mu, they would seek to help us. They were worried about what could happen to our little daughter as they did not want her to suffer. So, we agreed to make the formal apology. As the problem was urgent, Dong immediately did what he could to support Guang; this lessened the repercussions of the legal case without which we would have been in even worse trouble.

After the ceremony, my family did accept us back, but all the hurts from the past have left wounds. Today, I know that my family will always help us as we will help them. Mu often comes to our house to eat with us. She likes playing with her granddaughter, and the two of them have a close relationship. Mu is a devout Buddhist and goes to the local temple every month to worship. Whenever possible Guang drives her to the temple on the hill, and brings her back home when she has finished.

As our business is no more, we transferred our attention to cultivating the family land located outside the town. We planted rice, corn, vegetables, and sweet potatoes to feed ourselves and other family members. The rest we use to feed the pigs and chickens, which we then sell. Pig breeding is now a profitable business, as each sow can have as many as 12 piglets in a litter. As Mu previously raised pigs, she and Chun, give us lots of good advice. In these last years we have been able to extend our house three times, so it is now a large four-storeyed house. We have done all this for our daughter. We have tried to give her the best education possible, and I am pleased to say she is currently studying in high school and has a distinguished academic score.

I regret the years that Guang and I were in dispute with my family. I have learned that business and earning money are not everything in life, but you can't change the past. I am still ashamed of what we did especially with regards to Baba, but I am pleased that the family have accepted our daughter. Her cousins like her and she goes to visit them. Whenever I see them playing together I hope their generation will not be involved in as much trouble as ours was. It is said that it is only when you become a mother yourself that you realize all that your parents did for you. As for myself, I have learned the value of the family, and the importance of the land.

Notes

1. "Red"—To be a good member of the Chinese Communist Party.
2. In 1979, in Xiaogang village, Anhui Province, 18 households signed a contract with local cadres. The cadres secretly allowed farmers to produce by household and the farmers agreed that if the cadres were punished for this they would take care of their families.

CHAPTER 6

Chun's Story: First Son, Fourth Child

In China, it is sons, not daughters, who take responsibility for looking after parents when they are old. A proverb from the sage Mencius, one of the greatest philosophers of China, says, "There are three ways to be unfilial; having no sons is the worst."[1] Having no son is the worst because this means there is then no one to offer incense to the ancestors. If there is no son, a family often adopts the son of a brother or another close relative. My father had considered adoption, but my mother never wanted this. She was convinced that she would give birth to a son.

I am my family's first son and grew up with three elder sisters: Shun who was eight years older than I was, Shi who was six years older, and Hua who was four years older. Zhen told me that my birth brought great happiness to our family as everyone had wanted a boy. By the time I was born in 1961, the famine was past, and although the commune was still struggling to implement the new policies coming from Beijing, life was becoming more settled.

Even though I was a boy, my parents did not consider that I should be spoilt and treated differently from the girls. Most of the time I stayed with Grandma Xian and my sisters, and when I was only five I was required to do some housework. I started school when I was seven; Shun had finished primary school by this time and was working for the commune. Like our mother, Shun always encouraged me with my studies. Shi had also finished school and was at home helping Mu. So I joined my third sister Hua at our commune's primary school. I really enjoyed studying, and every semester

I would come top of my class, which pleased Mu and Shun. Mu always encouraged us all to work hard, and I remember how Shun and Shi would carry heavy loads of coal and work in the fields. I was also expected to help, which I did after returning home from school. Nevertheless, whenever I had a spare moment I would sit and read a book. Mu didn't mind me doing this as long as I had finished the housework I had been asked to do.

Our family was still quite poor although we did not go hungry as in earlier years. Most of my clothes were passed down from my elder sisters. At that time men and women, boys and girls all wore the blue Mao suit, and its shape and size could easily be altered. At school, we had to wear a shirt and red scarf, but my shirt was very worn and had been patched up before. I still remember the times when my younger brother Xia and I were laughed at by the other children because of the state of our shirts. Then one day Shi, who was learning to be a tailor, made both of us new shirts. Ah! We were so pleased with them, and walked proudly to school wearing them. We certainly took good care of those shirts as they had to last us a whole year.

When I was ten, the family had some great news. Shun had been chosen by our commune to attend college to become a teacher and all her fees would be paid. This meant that she moved out from the classification of a farmer and had an "iron rice bowl".[2] In old China, to have an "iron rice bowl" meant you had a permanent job, bringing you a steady income and good status. We were all proud of her as we knew she was a good student and a hard worker. Even so, I missed her when she went away. When she finished her studies a year-and-a-half later, she was appointed to the primary school in Heping village, which was not far away from our home. As she was a qualified teacher, paid by the government and not just a substitute-teacher, we all thought this was a great honour. It made me determined to do even better in my studies.

When I was 12, I started working with my father during the school holidays. Baba was eager for me to learn the skills of a vet from him just has he had learned them from his master. I went with Baba as he travelled around the villages, and stood by him to observe how he operated on the animals. As we travelled, Baba would tell me stories of his experiences, and his hope that in the future I would take over some of his customers in the villages. He told me that when we were visiting a family that I should always offer to do some housework. I would therefore often clean the floors or tidy the farm tools, so that the farmers came to like me. From Baba, I learned many things about the farmers and about veterinarian work.

I graduated from junior high school in 1976, and had passed the entrance examination for senior high school. Hua had gone on to senior high school, and would graduate in the following year, but it seemed that all she could do in the future was housework since all the universities were still closed. Apart from her, I had three younger brothers and sisters studying at school. My youngest brother, Dong, was only a year old. The family finances were really limited, and I knew that Baba hoped that I would take over as a local vet and make money to support the family. After working with Baba for seven months during the school holidays, I was able to do some simple operations myself. I continued working with Baba for another year and then started working on my own.

In the 1950s, there were no professional vets in the countryside, and the animal mortality rate was high. Then, in the 1960s, the commune established a veterinarian centre so that modern vaccines could be used. In the 1970s, the system was improved so that each village had a professional vet, like Baba, who was responsible for the prevention of epidemics and diseases. Every year the veterinarian centre insisted that all the villagers vaccinate their animals. Many of the farmers were at first suspicious of the new medicine and were reluctant to have their animals treated. But this was necessary because if the animals on one farm became infected it would quickly spread to all the village animals.

In the late 1970s, many of the youths who returned to the city from the countryside found it difficult to find jobs. For many of them the only way they could get a job was if their parent retired and they took over their job. This policy was called "replacement", and provided a way to solve recruitment problems in the city. Shun heard that this policy would be phased out in the following year with the reform of the employment system. She told this to Baba. The next day he asked his manager whether, when he retired, I could replace him. He was worried that with the change of policy I might not be able to find a job. In 1982, Baba retired, and I was appointed to a salaried position as a vet in the local station. The day I started work as an official vet rather than Baba's apprentice was a very special day for me, and both Baba and Mu were happy that I could take up the role. I remember wishing that I could inherit Baba's skill as well as his position when I became responsible for all Baba's old villages. Nowadays, the veterinarian station has entirely changed from what it was 25 years ago, but sometimes I can still feel Baba's presence during a hard day at the office.

After two years, I was sponsored by the station and given a full scholarship to go to college as its representative to learn scientific veterinarian management. I was pleased as although I had come to like helping the farmers, I wanted to learn more. Until this time, China's veterinarians merely learned their skills from the older generations as I had learned from Baba. The college I attended was one of the first large-scale village veterinary college training schemes, and I had the chance to learn scientific methods of animal care. I studied many subjects that Baba didn't know about such as animal nutrition, laboratory animal medicine, livestock environmental hygiene, and veterinary parasitology. I was eager to learn. The college had a library which was not big, but as I had never seen so many professional books before I spent almost all my spare time either reading or in the laboratory. I also met new friends at college including one of the most important people in my life, my course tutor, who later supported me in starting my own pig-feed business.

After a year, I graduated and immediately began practising as the only modern vet in my home area. I visited different villages to introduce the methods I studied in college. It was often hard because the farmers did not believe in these new methods; I became increasingly frustrated. One day Mu said to me, "Why don't you start with our family? We can do everything that you ask, and maybe we can become a model for your new methods." I thought that this was a great idea, and could see that Mu believed that education and knowledge was the best way to improve our way of life. So, our family began breeding a lot of pigs, and I was entrusted with the responsibility of looking after them. This gave me the chance to introduce some modern ideas. For example, traditionally pigs were only given cooked food and were kept in a dark room. I started feeding the pigs raw food and rebuilt the pigsty so that it was light and clean. When my younger brothers and sisters were home, I occasionally allowed the piglets to wander around the area, because they liked to look after them. As the pigs were kept fit and healthy, productivity increased. The local farmers could now see how successful modern methods were, and they started copying some of the things I was doing.

By now I was 25, and the family began to think that as the eldest son, the role of family head should soon move from Shun to me as the eldest son. My four younger siblings were still students and needed support. I knew that Shun had done a good job but the family should soon be my responsibility.

Then one day, without my knowledge, a local matchmaker came to Zhen and Cheng to discuss a possible marriage for me. None of the family had ever met the girl as she lived in another village. Zhen asked if the girl had any skills. The matchmaker said she was a tailor, like my second sister, and helped run her family's grocery shop. Mu recognized this was a good chance and possible match, so on that same day she set off on the two-hour walk to visit the store. She entered the shop intending to buy washing powder and salt, and casually started talking to the girl. Meanwhile I was busy at work and didn't know anything about the matchmaker's visit. When I returned home it was late evening, but I noticed that Mu looked mysterious. I asked her, "What was the matter?" She told me that a matchmaker had just visited them and spoke to them about a cadre's daughter. Not knowing anything about the girl Mu said she had gone to see her. As soon as she saw the girl, she knew she would be a good wife for me. I asked her, "What so impressed you about this girl?" She said, "She has a good figure and is kind; most importantly she is a skilful tailor and can earn cash." I don't know how Mu could have gleaned all this in such a short conversation, but I knew Mu was smart and experienced. I sometimes think that a woman's intuition is like magic!

Zhen informed the matchmaker that the family would like to move to the next stage in the marriage arrangements. As the first son, I realized that for me marriage would never be merely an individual decision, and the whole family would want to be in agreement with it. I went to visit the girl's family and to see what Lan was like for myself. I quickly saw that she had a nice kind personality and was a hard worker just as Mu had said. She was also good looking, so I was happy for the arrangements to proceed. The family did not want to have a disagreement like the one which had occurred when my third sister Hua wanted to marry. Once the arrangements had begun, I started visiting some of the farmers in that area to get more customers, but also to allow me to visit Lan and her family. I purposely would make a detour to pass by Lan's home, and would stop by to ask them for a cup of tea. I could see that Lan was always happy when I visited. After the tea, I would offer to do any jobs to help the family. You can see how I benefited from the training Baba had given me! Lan's mother and sisters-in-law were happy because they thought that I not only had a good job, but I also helped with the housework. Nowadays when Lan talks with our daughter about marriage she says that she appreciated my willingness to help. We married in 1988.

After Shi's wedding, Shun had argued that we should no longer have expensive weddings for the other children as there were so many of us in our family. In hindsight, I can see that this was a wise decision. However, Lan's father planned a big banquet and invited many of his family and friends to celebrate. As our family was still poor, we planned to have a small and modest celebration with only family members. As I didn't know if Lan's family would be happy with this plan, I was cautious when I proposed this idea to her father. I was relieved that he understood, and said that we should do things in terms of our financial situation. He even added that it was not necessary for us to give any gifts to his family so as to reduce the pressure on our family. After I told my parents this, Mu said Lan's family had shown us great respect, and that the only way to repay this is to love Lan with all our hearts.

The day we married, we held a formal ritual in our living hall. As tradition dictates, my parents sat in the centre of the hall with our family members around them. Lan and I stood side-by-side opposite Mu and Baba. We bowed first to heaven and earth, second to our ancestors, third to my parents, and finally we bowed to each other. After this, Lan was accepted into our family, and from then on, she called my parents Baba and Mu.

In those days, two types of gifts were given to couples getting married. The first were those given by friends, which included pieces of cloth, clothes, towels, shoes, and bowls—all items needed to help them set up their new home. The second type came from the girl's family, usually a financial contribution for the couple—what in English is called a dowry. Because Lan's father had a senior position, and his two elder brothers were also cadres, they gave Lan a substantial gift. The wives of Lan's brothers were local girls, but they didn't receive so many gifts from their families. I am sure they were a little jealous of the gift Lan received from their father-in-law, but they could not object as they had only recently married into the family.

After the marriage, Lan came to live with me in Jin'e where she continued to work as a tailor. Mu would often say that I should treat Lan well as she not only had a sewing machine, but was also a good tailor. She said that it is difficult to find such a hard-working virtuous wife. We lived together in the old house, but Lan worked in the new house the family had built in the town centre. Because she was skilful and had money to buy cloth, she was able to recruit three apprentices, including my young sister Kai. Lan was a hard worker, and a good organizer. She would start work early in the morning and return home late. Nevertheless, she would help to prepare dinner and did some housework. Lan's coming assisted our family both in the work she did and the finances she contributed. In particular, my young sister became close to her.

In the year I married, it was agreed that I was old enough to take on responsibility for the family. I also set up a store in the new house with the aim of selling quality pig fodder. I taught Lan about the fodder, so she could sell it when I was out visiting the farmers. I taught the farmers the best way to feed their pigs and chickens. Knowing me from the years I had worked with Baba and knowing also that I had been professionally trained, they trusted me and the advice I gave. They were therefore happy to go to my store to buy the fodder for their animals.

In 1987, the central government introduced some new policies that began to influence agricultural methods in our country. I taught the farmers the new methods of animal management, which included the current practices of vaccinating their animals against various diseases. We also started selling these vaccines in the store in Jin'e. Through hard work, both our businesses were doing well.

The following year Lan became pregnant and we were so happy with this news. Mu had given birth to all her children at home, but by the late of 1980s, many women gave birth in the local hospital. I wanted Lan to give birth in the town hospital, so she could have proper care. I must admit I was somewhat disappointed that the child she bore was a girl. At that time, all rural couples wanted their first child to be a boy, and with the introduction of the one-child policy, it looked as though I would never have a son. However, before the actual birth Shun had called a family meeting and told us all that as this child was born to the first son it would be the first of the new generation through the sons. As such the child should be treated in terms of the new perspectives of our nation. So, whatever the sex of the child, the child should be lovingly cared for and given a good education. I am pleased to say we all did this.

There is a tradition in China called "sitting the month".[3] It involves the new mother staying at home for a month to recover from childbirth. During this month, she must follow many rules including not drinking cold water, eating heavy tasty food, salt, and not even eating raw fruit and vegetables. In particular, the new mother needs to wear a hat to protect her head. It was said that these rules were aimed at restoring the balance of the new mother's body after childbirth. Nowadays, there are many debates and discussion about whether these traditions are good or not, but at that time most mothers followed these rules. Young mothers had a hard time following these traditions. After a week, Lan's relatives came to visit us and they brought many gifts for Lan and the baby. Baba and Mu treated Lan very well, and the little girl grew up loving her grand-parents.

It is a traditional custom in our family that when a new child is born to invite a fortune-teller to come to divine something about their future. The practice is called *Wu Xing* or the "Five Elements", because it involves the five dominant elements: metal, wood, fire, earth, and water. This fivefold scheme is used to explain a wide variety of phenomena in many fields in order to establish harmony and balance. When the diviner cast the child's fortune, he found a shortage of the element water, and so suggested we name her Yu, which means "rain" so as to bring the elements into balance.

Although Cheng had retired from the official position as a vet, and was not scientifically trained, his years of practical experience meant that he was still very skilful in many tasks. He therefore continued to travel around among the farmers helping them with their animals, and in this way, he continued to contribute to the family income. Often farmers would give him gifts of food, which he took back home. These were good days.

Then in 1993, we were confronted with a major problem that came as a shock to both of us. Lan found that she was pregnant again. She wanted to give birth to the child, which she hoped would be a boy. However, as the one-child policy was being enforced, I knew that if Lan gave birth to the child I would most likely lose my job. And if I lost my job what would happen to my younger brothers and sisters who were still at college or high school? It was a bad time for us both. Lan wanted to keep the child, while I wanted her to have an abortion. I know that this was a situation many couples had to face, but knowing this does not make the decision any easier. On the one hand, you want to be loyal to state policy, and on the other hand, you want to have another child especially a son. Some couples paid the big fine for disobeying the directive, others had their child adopted by someone else in their family, and still others found ways of hiding their child from the authorities. But I was a cadre in the town, and I didn't want to lose my official job. I needed to follow the rules, and so I asked Lan to have an abortion.

Reluctantly Lan agreed. On leaving hospital, Lan didn't want to come home with me, but went to stay with her parents. I felt sad and ashamed about the whole event, but could see no alternative. After a couple of days, I went to encourage Lan to return home, but she didn't want to talk with me and wanted to stay longer with her parents. After another two weeks, my young sister and I went to persuade Lan, and after a little while she did come home with us. Both of us were hurt by the decision we had to make, and it took time for the hurt to heal.

When Lan returned home, she found the business was going well despite her absence and we were still making money. We decided to concentrate all our attention on our business and try our best to support our little daughter. We also decided to build a new house on the remaining plot of land near the town centre. At that time, my former college tutor started an agricultural business; we joined his team and became a branch of his company.

That same year another tragedy occurred: Baba became ill, and I had to take him to the city hospital. Baba did not have health insurance, and the doctor told us that treatment would be costly. We asked the doctor to give Baba the best treatment, and the family would pay. After a month, Baba recovered and came back home. Lan gave up her work as a tailor to concentrate on the agricultural business that had become very busy, and since she was working from home she could also look after Baba. One morning, Lan heard a sound from the toilet and ran to see what had happened. She found Baba lying on the floor in a coma. She shouted for me and we quickly called a doctor. Although he did his best, Baba left us that afternoon. We buried him in a tomb set on the side of a hill looking down over the valley.

In 2002, I was appointed to an administrative position responsible for pig farming in the whole of the local area. That same year vets were no longer required to visit every farmer. We only did this when a farmer asked us to come and castrate a pig, for example, or when pigs were about to be slaughtered or sold out of the village when we would check for any diseases. With the continuing improvement of the country's economy, people could afford to eat more meat. Farmers were therefore eager to rear more pigs for slaughter; the authorities however were concerned that this was done in a scientific way, so I was asked to oversee the slaughter and sale of all pigs in the county. My responsibilities included overseeing and recording the slaughter of all the animals and ensuring farmers paid their tax. It was an important position as it helped the whole community; I took it very seriously, and wanted to avoid any hint of corruption.

My elder sister, Shi was also in the business of selling agricultural products. One day she visited me in my office on the top floor of our apartment. She asked me to do her a favour and give her some tax relief. While I knew that some cadres did give family members advantages I told Shi, that because she was my sister, some people would take note of how we worked together, so we had to do everything strictly according to the law otherwise I'll be criticized. I thought that Shi knew this of course but she always liked to make a profit. When I said she would be charged exactly the same rate as all the other farmers she got angry with me and stormed out of my office. This is an on-going difficulty for all cadres; you are pulled between loyalty to one's family and honesty and integrity in one's duties to the Party and the State.

The following year Shi came to me again. The veterinarian station where I live is next door to her house, and Shi noticed that part of the veterinary station's land wasn't being used. She wanted to move the boundary wall so as to make use of the land. Shi knew that the land belonged to the station not me personally, and so she should have known that I could not give her permission to do this. I thought that I had made my position quite clear to her before. Once again, she left in anger and would no longer speak to me. I think from then on all the family realized that I wanted to be honest and avoid any hint of corruption. From then on, nobody in the family came to seek any favours from me due to my position. Lan told our daughter Yu something of what had happened, and said that although we are no longer on speaking terms with Shi, she should always be polite to her auntie and speak to her whenever she met her in the street. We had decided that this was a disagreement that should not pass on to the next generation.

The temptation to make easy money is an issue that many government officials face. I remember on one occasion a businessman came to visit me at my house, and we had a pleasant time together. After he left, I discovered a packet of money. I quickly rang him and told him to come and collect the money at once. He did return, and with some shame and confusion left with the money. This was a practice amongst many who were seeking a special favour such as speeding up a particular decision. Every year I was appraised by the country authorities, and I am pleased to say that I became recognized as being an excellent official. I always say that it is only by being honest that I can sleep well at night and so have a happy life.

Changing policies continued to affect business in the villages. Many farmers went to the cities as migrant workers, so less farming was being done. Some of the large agricultural companies also began exploring opportunities to sell their products not only in the towns but even in the smaller villages. They started setting up sales points in each village, so farmers could easily phone to have fodder delivered directly to their farms. My younger brother Xia became one of these agents. However, Lan and I found the competition from the major corporations led to the gradual decline of our business, and eventually we closed it in 2007. Fortunately, by this time all of my brothers and sisters had jobs and were married which meant that Lan didn't have to work anymore. She was happy to be a full-time housewife.

I must admit that when our daughter was little I didn't spend much time with her; I left it to Lan to look after her. Over the years, I began to like the child more and more, and by the time she was a teenager I had a great love for her. She was kind and helpful like her mother. Lan always wanted Yu to do well at school, even though I said she should not pressurize her too much—high grades are not everything in life. We decided to send her to a good boarding school so that she would excel in her studies. After she left, I felt the house was empty, and I was sad that I had given so little time to her when she was a little girl. So now, whenever she comes home, I make a point of cooking special food for her—which is something that I would never normally do. Yu was initially surprised that I made the effort to cook for her, but I think she soon realized it was my way of expressing my love for her. When Yu had to return to school, Lan would break the shells of walnuts so she only had to carry the kernels. I know that it might sound silly, but I liked helping Lan with the task. The first time Yu saw me doing this with her Mom, she was puzzled and exclaimed, "Daddy you are helping Mom to break the shells." "Yes, for you," I said with a big smile. I still remember how Yu looked at me with a big grin and said "OK, OK." In that instant, I felt a new depth of love between us. Now when she is home, Lan and I talk about all sorts of things with her; I now understand Yu all the more. I think that in recent years the three of us have grown closer together.

Over the years, it has become a family custom that at New Year we all spend the night of the new moon together. Baba introduced this family tradition. All the family members would gather at my house where Zhen lived. We'd play games late into the night and, after a brief nap, get up at about 5 a.m. Unfortunately this meant that Lan had to get up at 3 a.m. to prepare breakfast for everyone. Before breakfast, we'd go up onto the flat roof to light candles and burn paper money as an offering to the ancestors. Then we'd eat breakfast together. This could take as long as four hours until daylight had fully come. During the meal we chatted about the past year, and plan for the year to come. After the children went out to play and our wives were tidying up, the four of us brothers would go into a separate room to discuss the family situation. This is a time when each one of us could share our feelings honestly and face up to any problems. In this way, we try to support each other and the family as a whole. It is a good time!

In October 2009, China established the Chinese Veterinary Medical Association (CVMA) whose stated aim is to assist in the modernization of Chinese veterinary science. As a consequence of this, every village now has a trained vet who is responsible for looking after the village animals. If any farmer needs help, he can directly call the vet who will go to treat the animals on their farm. This is a big difference from 20 years ago when I first began working with Baba. In 2012, although veterinarians are predominantly employed by the government, there was a shift to private practice and research. Textbooks are more and more up-to-date and the ratio of students and faculty is going down. Although things aren't perfect, with the establishment of the CVMA, China's younger generation of veterinarians are hoping for a new era of professionalism. For many students, academics, and practitioners the CVMA represents the hope of uniting the profession, raising standards to the highest common denominator, and improving clinical practice.

In recent years, all my brothers have left our town to work in cities, but I still work in the vet station in Jin'e, and Mu still lives with us. My daughter too now works in the city, but she comes back to stay with us for several days during her holiday. Lan is kind in looking after Mu especially when I am travelling away from home. Lan likes to invite Mu to go social activities in the area as she thinks that this is good for her health. Today, dancing in the public square is popular in all Chinese communities. After dinner many middle-aged and retired women get together in their community square to dance. Every time I pass by the square at dance time, I see Mu sitting at the side looking at Lan with her gracious moves. As a son and a husband, I really appreciate their close relationship. I hope life can continue to be one that is peaceful and loving.

Notes

1. Mencius Readings – 4A.26 Mencius said, "There are three forms of unfiliality, and bearing no heirs is the worst." Opinions are mixed as to what Mencius could have been referring to as the other two forms.
2. The system of employment from the 1950s was known as the "iron rice bowl", centrally administered wages (the "iron wage"), and state-controlled appointment, and promotion of managerial staff (the "iron chair").
3. "sitting the month", 坐月子 Pinyin: *zuoyuezi*.

CHAPTER 7

Xia's Story: Second Son

I was born in 1967, the sixth child of Zhen and Cheng. Like my older brother, Chun, I went to school when I was six years old. My teacher was a former soldier who wasn't good at writing Chinese characters. Sometimes, I would write the characters as he had taught us, but Chun would look at them and say that they were wrong. Chun would then show me what he thought were the right ones. Whenever this happened, we always asked Shun what she thought was correct. Even though my class teacher was not good with textbooks, he was good at acting and he brought a lot of fun to the classroom. In the mornings, I went to school, but in the afternoons, I looked after the cows for the commune. I had little free time; neither did my brothers and sisters who were always busy with homework or housework. Nevertheless, we looked after each other and had fun together. We had nicknames for each other and we would tease one another. Childhood was a happy time for me.

When I was nine, I started farming with Mu, which I really enjoyed. I learned how to plant crops like sweet potatoes. I planted a small vine and made sure it was regularly fertilized. After five months, the leaves of the vine had spread, covering the whole field; when we cut them back, we dug in the soil and found big clusters of sweet potatoes. The vine leaves too provided good food for both people and the pigs. During harvest season, I remember my hands were often covered in the juice of sweet potatoes. In those days, sweet potato was often our family's main food—sweet potato soup, sweet potato porridge, steamed sweet potato, and stewed sweet potato. Chun says we even cooked the leaves of sweet potato to make another dish to eat with the sweet potato roots! Nowadays, he never wants to eat sweet potato ever again.

One thing I remember that really helped farmers at that time, 1977, was the introduction of a new hybrid strain of rice, which increased our harvest by 20%! Where previously we got a yield of 600 kg per Mu (666 square metres), we now got 750 kg. Mum said that in the 1950s, some people boasted that they got a yield of 10,000 kg, which was a ridiculous joke. Anyway, the increase from 600 to 750 kg greatly benefited both farmers and the nation as a whole. Everyone was so grateful for the work of Yuan Longping,[1] the scientist who developed the variety; we called him the father of hybrid rice. He was greatly respected and considered a hero by all farmers. But guess what, in 2016, I had the privilege of meeting him at a conference. Wasn't that amazing! By then, he was already an old man.

In the mornings, Mu insisted that we got up early—around six o'clock, when the cocks in our yard crow three times. In the wintertime, Qiu and Dong often tried to stop the cocks from crowing but they always failed. After getting up, we had to read books. In the winter we used to sit together around the charcoal fire, and in the summer we would sit together under the eaves. The house was full of the sound of children reading aloud, and sometimes this led to arguments because our loud reading annoyed each other. My younger sister Kai was always the last one to join us and seemed to have a different excuse every time. Then, we all spent another 40 minutes doing housework, taking it in turns to cook breakfast. My main duty was to fetch water from the village well for our family to use and for the pigs to drink. At around eight o'clock, we'd all rush to school one behind the other along a long, narrow raised path between the fields, and then, after turning a corner, race along the dirt road going to town.

The happiest time in the whole year was the Spring Festival when there was no homework, no endless chores, no scolding from parents but nice meals and free time. It is when we say farewell to the old year and welcome the new, and it is also the longest holiday. In the twelfth lunar month, people eat "*naba* porridge", which is rice porridge with nuts and dried fruit. From then on our family would begin to prepare for the New Year celebration. One of the most exciting things was the slaughter of the pig we'd reared; we called it "the year pig". After the commune school moved to the new town at the beginning of the 1980s, the playground of the old site was used by the local residents to dry the grain and corn collected from their fields. Neighbours also used it as a place to slaughter pigs for the Spring Festival. A cooking range was built in a corner of the playground, where water was boiled to clean the pigs. For two weeks before the New Year, the screams of the pigs begging for their lives to be saved echoed over the playground every day.

On the day we slaughtered our pig, with the help of a neighbour who was a butcher, all of us brothers chased the pig out of the sty and tried to hold it still for the butcher. Chun, Qiu, Dong, and I pulled and pushed the pig. As it weighed more than 100 kg, it was very difficult. Maybe the pig realized what would happen to it when it saw the boiled water and the blood on the ground in the playground! We usually met with desperate resistance from the pig and had to ask neighbours to help us pin him down so that the butcher could kill it. Then we cleaned the pig with boiled water before the butcher cut up the carcass. This always made me think of the proverb "Dead pig is not afraid of hot water"; a metaphor meaning someone is thick skinned. We often used it for each other when we made the same mistakes.

That night, the family would invite relatives to have a big meal with us. Baba was a good cook and made a special soup with the blood. He would also usually cut a little bit of each part of the pig, including both the meat and the internal organs. On the following day, he would make sausages and bacon, which we hung in the smoke to dry. Baba also made fried rice and made steamed yellow rice cakes. In the 24th day of the last month of the lunar calendar, tradition says that the kitchen god goes to heaven to celebrate Chinese New Year with his leader and to report what has happened in the family and community during the last year. We therefore prepared small dishes of food and a small bottle of alcohol to give to the kitchen god in our home. We asked him to speak nicely of our family and community and for us all to have a happy and peaceful year. Perhaps our most important request was that we would have a good harvest in the coming year. The kitchen god would then be welcomed back on New Year's Eve. Nowadays only Grandma, Shun, and Chun's family continue to do this ceremony; the third generation doesn't bother with it at all.

On New Year's Eve, which was called *Shousui* (守岁), we would make two lanterns and hang them under the overhang of the roofs. We also posted red paper couplets on either side of our gateway; we could either buy these or write them ourselves. The couplets usually welcome the coming New Year and wish blessings on it. We also posted pictures of the door gods on the main door of the house. There are various categories of door gods like "drive evil spirits out" or "pray for happiness"; some are named after famous generals from ancient Chinese history. That night we would stay up late, sometimes all night, let off fireworks, and burn incense and paper money for the ancestors. The first month of the lunar year is called *Zhengyue* (正月). Usually, the children were given some money as a New Year gift from friends of our parents.

During the day of New Year Eve, all the members of our family came together for a banquet. Some families have their festival meal either at lunchtime or in the evening, but Baba said it was most auspicious to have it at breakfast, as the sunshine was brightest and would mean that the coming days would always be bright. It was the best meal of the whole year when we ate pork and chicken dishes. Mu also steamed some rice in a small bowl, which she kept until the following New Year's Eve; this was the "over year rice".

On New Year's Day, we usually ate rice balls with sweet bean curd inside. In Chinese, a circle means completeness, so having rice balls at our first meal meant we would have a good year. After breakfast, we would go for a walk in the direction Baba said would be auspicious for us as a family. When we met friends, we would call out "*Gongxifacai*" (恭喜发财)—"May you be happy and prosperous." On that day, we couldn't throw water away or sweep the floor because if you did, you would sweep away good fortune and prosperity. Whenever someone knocked on our door, they gave us a traditional greeting and a paper portrait of the god of wealth and we gave them a little money. The amount would always have to be 4, double 6, or 12. You might wonder if these have a special meaning. Yes, they do—4 means make a fortune for four seasons; double 6 and 12 mean lucky for 12 months.

On the second or third day of the holiday, the family went to our ancestral tomb to set off firecrackers and burn paper money. We would also leave small dishes of food and a cup of alcohol at the tomb. Mu said these small dishes were for our ancestors, and we would be blessed if we ate a portion of them, so we always did. On the eighth day, the temples in the towns would set up poles and hang rows of lanterns on a rope between them. This was called "sky light"—the aim was said to avoid misfortunes and difficulties in the coming year.

The fifteenth of *Zhengyue* is the last day of the Spring Festival and is called *Yuanxiao* or "Lantern Festival". At night, people played with dragon lanterns, which were believed "to burn mildew away and bring a bonanza". As the dragon lanterns went along the streets, people would light firecrackers to welcome them. The whole village was filled with the sound of firecrackers and people enjoying the last day of the holiday. They were happy times. The following day, we would once again start working in the fields hoping for a good harvest to come.

In the summer of 1985, my family decided to build a new house in the town centre on land that we had been given. To save money, we did much of the construction work ourselves. For the first two months, I lived day and night at the site to prevent anyone from stealing the building materials. I can tell you, living there was hot, and there were many mosquitos that kept me awake during the night. Even today when I see the house I still feel that all the hard work was worth it. That house reminds me of many of the events of my youth.

Once the house was finished, we bought a television and a washing machine. The TV was a 17-inch black and white set, and we erected an aerial in the yard behind the house. At that time, there were only six channels, which broadcast only between 7:00 a.m. and 11:30 p.m. In the summer, we would move the TV out of the house into the yard where it was cooler. Often neighbours would come after dinner, bringing their own stools, and join us for watching TV; sometimes, there would be as many as 20 people around the TV set. When the wind blew, the aerial would shake and the image and sound would immediately be distorted; Qiu would always jump up to hold the pole and repeatedly ask, "Is this alright?" and several people answered at the same time, "OK" or "Hold it," until the wind stopped. Unfortunately, as the pole was behind the house, he couldn't even see the TV!

After I graduated from high school in 1986, I started working in our fields with Mu and also helped my elder brother, Chun, with his veterinarian work. After the passing of the Rural Household Contract Responsibility System, farmers could benefit from what they grew in their own fields, so everyone worked with new enthusiasm. The busiest time of the year was summer because both corn and rice were ready to harvest. It was hot; the temperature usually being around 35 degrees. We wore straw hats on our heads and boots on our feet. After cutting the rice stalks, we would lay them flat in the fields. Then we prepared a big bucket lined with split bamboo rods where we would thresh the unshelled rice. The split bamboo rods helped prevent the rice from bouncing out of the bucket. This is the traditional way of threshing rice in our area of China, but it took a lot of hard, manual work. Often, we would spend all day bending down, collecting the unshelled rice. I still remember how our backs ached at the end of the day. There is an old saying, "Facing the earth, back to sky, working with busy hands". It is a portrayal of our life in those days. In the evening, we would carry the unshelled rice back home where we spread it out on a mat to dry. If the sky was overcast or rainy, it was difficult to separate the rice from the husk and the harvest could be spoiled.

After we had dried the rice grains, we would take the rice required for tax (*Gongliang*)[2] to the public grain store. The amount of grain tax depended on the acreage each family farmed. When we arrived at the centre, the inspectors would first check the quality of the rice. They would grab a handful of rice and choose one grain to bite and taste. If the quality wasn't good enough or it wasn't sufficiently dry, the farmer would need to spread the rice out on the flat area outside the centre until it was dry. In the beginning of 2006, the central government cancelled the agriculture tax so farmers no longer had to pay the grain tax. Since the authorities had required the grain tax ever since the time of the Shang dynasty,[3] you can imagine what great news this was for the farmers; everyone was delighted.

In 1990, when I was 23, a friend of my young sister recommended me for a job at the local Jin'e government as a temporary official responsible for the implementation of the one-child policy in the area. This policy advocated that couples should only have one child, and strongly recommended late marriage and childbirth. In the beginning of the 1980s, it was first implemented as a temporary measure but soon became fixed policy. Thereafter, billboards on village house walls throughout the country carried slogans like "Give birth to fewer children, plant more trees and rear more pigs," and "In order to improve the development of China give birth to only one child."

Some families were allowed to apply to have a second child. These included farmers working in distant rural areas if their first child was a daughter or was disabled, and people from ethnic minorities who lived in the countryside. If a family broke the regulation, they were subject to a hefty fine, which varied from province to province. The one-child policy was managed by the National Population and Family Planning Commission under the central government from 1981.

As couples could only have one child, they preferred to have a son. In the countryside, many farmers who didn't work in government departments had two children, keeping the second child secret. The government attempted to educate parents about the value of daughters, but it did little good. As I came from a farming family, I knew how eager my parents were to have a son for many years before Chun was born. I deeply understood those people who broke the regulations, but I had to do my job fairly and according to the government's requirements. I can tell you it was not easy.

As families had fewer children, they invested more in their education whether the child was a boy or a girl. The one-child policy was formally phased out in 2015. I only worked at this job for a short time as it was hard, and I preferred farming with Zhen.

At this time, it was becoming more popular for families to divide their property between the sons. For ordinary families, the practice was that when a son married, his bride joined him in his parent's home. They had their own bedroom but shared the rest of the facilities. If the family has several sons, after each son married, the new couple would start their own family and live on their own. Wealthy families would divide their property after all their sons had married, and then they discussed who would be responsible for the elderly parents. This meant that responsibility was shifted from a father to the son and his own small family. As daughters married into another family, it was assumed that their husband's family would provide for their sons and their wives. This practice of dividing the family is called *fenjia* that means "divide family".

There are usually three ways in which sons can look after their parents when they are elderly. Both parents live with one of the sons, while the other sons provide them with pocket money and rice. In the second way, the parents move between the sons, spending a period with each one. Third, the parents separate and each one goes to live with a different son. *Fenjia* was a major decision for any Chinese family to take. Some families invited the elders of the clan and the village head to come as witnesses. All the men are blood relatives, but the women have married in from other families. Often the women are not included in the division, as they would argue that they should be given different pieces of furniture, land, and responsibilities. Today, with the planned birth policy and the development of the economy, *fenjia* rarely occurs.

In the case of our family, there were five children living at home: Chun who was married, me, and three younger children who were at college or high school. When Chun married, he felt he was responsible as the eldest son for all his younger siblings so he continued to live in the family home. *Fenjia* was an important decision for us, but it was necessary because our family was big and the boys were growing up. We made the family division in 1990.

On that day, the whole family gathered in the old house and Shun presided over the arrangements. After considerable discussion, the family decided to make three packages: the first was half the new house and the care of Baba, the second was half the new house and the care of Zhen, and the third was the old house with no responsibilities. The packages included many items, including those as small as the as-yet-unborn piglets in the mother pig. We also agreed that we would decide who took which package by taking lots. Shun wrote the three packages on three bits of paper and placed them face down on the table. With all the family members present, the youngest son was allowed to be the first to take one of the papers, then it was my turn. Chun took the remaining paper.

Chun had half the new house with the responsibility of Baba, while I had the other half of the house and was responsible for looking after Zhen. Chun and I had also taken on the responsibility of paying Dong's college tuition fees. The third son, Qiu, got the old house without any family responsibilities. As Zhen and Cheng still lived and worked in the old house, all the furniture and animals went with it.

Chun then moved into part of the new house in the town centre; all the other members of the family remained in the old house. Zhen and Cheng are responsible for the farm but would be helped by any children who were home and available. Shun arranged for a document to be produced to show that I owned property.

One day in 1996 one of my colleagues came to talk to me about her niece, Lian. She told me how Lian helped her father with his business and went on to say that they were looking for a suitable husband for her. She asked me if I thought that Lian would be a suitable partner for me. Wow! That came as a surprise, so I asked my family about this suggestion. Lian was five years younger than me, and our families knew each other. In fact, I walked by her house every day as I went to work at the government office. I used to see her setting up her stall early in the morning, and if we met, we would greet each other.

The family thought that this could be a good proposal. Shun, who was experienced in these things, asked a local matchmaker to visit the girl's parents and see if the family was open to a possible proposal. Much to our surprise, the approach was rejected by the girl's mother. We later found out that the reason for the refusal was that the mother was a close friend of the daughter-in-law of Baba's former master, the vet. This family was the one that had conflicts with Baba, and although this had all happened many years before, our two families had never had much contact. When the mother discussed this possible proposal with her friend, she told some lies about us that made the mother reject the proposal. We didn't know about this until later and thought that the reason the proposal had been rejected was that they considered our family did not come up to scratch. I must admit I was very disappointed by the refusal.

After half a year, the girl's family were still looking for a suitable match for Lian. Her auntie was Shun's friend and colleague and knew me and my family well. At a family party, the topic of Lian's marriage came up in the discussion. The auntie thought I would be a good husband for Lian and said she was willing to talk to her. She explained to Shun that the problem had arisen as a result of an old argument with Baba. Shun asked me what I felt about the auntie's proposal. Of course, I was very pleased because Lian was a beautiful young woman and I certainly wanted to get to know her better. Shun wondered who would be a suitable matchmaker and then realized that the girl's auntie would be ideal. She was delighted to be asked to take on the role. As a result, Lian's family agreed to start formal wedding procedures.

I immediately started preparing appropriate gifts for Lian's family, and Shi and Chun helped me with the finance. By then, I was 28 and considered mature enough to marry, so I hoped the marriage would be soon, but the day had to be an auspicious one. It so happened that the following year was considered an unlucky year in which to marry, so everyone thought that we should marry that very year—1997. Although Lian and I were very happy with this, before Lian's family decided on the marriage date, her father wanted to see the property documents as proof that I actually owned part of the house.

On Lian's marriage, her family gave her a substantial dowry of 4200 RMB. At that time, this was a big dowry in our town. When her father handed me the money, he said it shouldn't be used for any other purpose than for Lian and me to start a new business. Over the years, I have had a good relationship with Lian's father. He supervised me when I wanted to start our business and taught me to make sure that I had all the necessary formal documents, especially when doing a big business deal.

After we married, my father-in-law invited me to work as a manager in his factory, which made stone aggregate. Lian continued with the clothing business she started soon after she graduated from high school, now based in our new house. I learned a lot about business from my father-in-law and also from Lian who was always supportive and patient. I remember in the following year, one of Lian's relatives argued with Shun; Shun became so angry and ended up slapping her face. When the relative told Lian, she defended her sister-in-law, who she knew was a reasonable person. When

Lian told me about this, I was pleased that she now felt such loyalty to my family.

By this time, an increasing number of shops had opened in our town, encouraged by the market that was now held every three days. The government began investing money in road construction and new power lines; as a result, many larger businesses came to the area such as coal mining, power stations, brick factories, and building companies.

This business activity encouraged the local farmers to start planting cash crops like tobacco and silkworm mulberry bushes. The regional government chose some hard-working families of good education to be recognized as "a model household of science and technology". This practice helped to speed up the adoption of new agricultural technologies. My family was always in the first group of households to use these new practices. With every new technological innovation, agricultural experts were made available to give the farmers the necessary training and services. When the farmers saw how the model households started making money, they were eager to adopt the new technology themselves. Farmers' income started rising rapidly and people began improving their houses and bought many new things. These were exciting times for the area.

After a year, Lian gave birth to a son, which delighted the whole family. As my elder brother, Chun, had a daughter, our child was the first boy of the third generation of Cheng's family name, which meant that the family line would continue through him. We named him Hai, which means "sea", and hoped he would grow up to be broadminded and open to new ideas. It was actually my youngest brother, Dong, then studying at college who suggested it.

Lian and I were both busy with our businesses, which made it difficult for us to look after our son. Lian decided to reduce her business responsibilities so as to look after him herself, and my sister-in-law, Lan, who was our neighbour offered to help. In 1999, when Hai was two years old, Lian and I decided to move to Wenxing city in order to further develop our businesses. Lian's older sister already had a good business there and told us that there were many good business opportunities. Hai was then old enough to attend full-time kindergarten. In our first few years in the city, we lacked personal connections and at times were short of funds. In order to increase the sale of agricultural products, I needed to build a network of farmers who trusted me. I did this by riding on a motorcycle to different counties and towns. I suppose over those years I drove thousands of miles. Occasionally, I would get soaked in the heavy rain. We also moved house almost every year, either for cheaper rent or better business. Whatever difficulties I encountered, I always tried my best to overcome them, but it still placed a cost on my family. To this day, I remember when my son showed me his first writing assignment in which he said that his family were always moving from one place to another and his biggest wish was to have a fixed residence. I was sad to read this, but like Grandma Xian said, "This is the life and we have to fight for a better one."

In our second year in the city, a law was passed, allowing agricultural seeds to be sold by private businesses. When my youngest sister, Kai, heard about this, she immediately seized the new business opportunity of selling seed direct to the farmers. Kai had studied at agricultural college and so had good knowledge of modern agricultural methods. I too was from a farming background and familiar with the farmers' requirements. Lian and I began selling seed directly to the farmers, and we expanded the business to include the sale of fertilizer.

With the expansion of the business, I was able to sign a number of good contracts with major companies based in the provincial city, which gave us the sole right to sell their products in Wenxing county. Lian and I also attended training courses offered by these companies that helped us manage our business better, sell products, and attract more customers. These ideas not only expanded our thinking but also gave us the skills to expand our business into other areas. We bought several shops and recruited salespeople and a professional accountant.

In 2005, as an agent for one particular brand, I sold thousands of tons of fodder. At the end of the year, the company awarded me a seven-seater van, which greatly improved my mobility, as I no longer had to worry about bad weather. Then, the government initiated the One Hundred Village Project in Wenxing county in order to stimulate the local economy. The plan was to encourage the city chain stores to expand to distant villages. The goal was that 50% of villages and 70% of towns would have a store selling fertilizer, seeds, and other agricultural products. The farmers could then take advantage of an interest-free loan to increase their use of these products. Fortunately, I was able to take advantage of this opportunity and became one of the first agencies in the project. In 2007, we set up our own company and bought a three-storey building as our company headquarters. By 2009, in the whole of China, there were 360,000 chain stores in villages covering 71% of towns and 44% of villages. This programme met the requirements of the farmers and produced many new employment opportunities in the area.

During the project, I bought a four-wheel drive SUV, which made travel much more convenient and efficient. At this time, my youngest brother, Dong, had graduated from college and was appointed as an official after working as a teacher for several years. Because he was hard working and naturally bright, he was promoted as an outstanding official. Dong was able to give me advice about the new government policies, which provided us with further opportunities to expand our business.

It was as a result of all the travelling I had to do that made me think about my son's future. The news media often reported traffic accidents in which often somebody was killed. In 2005, the only child of one of my friends was seriously injured in an accident and later died. I realized that Lian and I should have another child. Because we were not government officials, it was easier for us to do this, although we would have to pay a fine which, at that time, amounted to 7000 RMB. At first, Lian wasn't enthusiastic because it would cause her too much work and we were already very busy. However, I persisted and Lian finally changed her mind. We both hoped to have a daughter because we think daughters are often closer to their parents, especially when they get older. So, when in 2007 Lian gave birth to a second son, we were a little bit disappointed. We named him Xuan. After the birth, I paid the fine, which was a considerable sum for most people, but the success of our business enabled us to make the payment, and so the baby was registered on our family's *hukou* documents.

When our oldest son completed primary school in Wenxing, he was offered a place at one of the best middle schools in the whole province, but it was 500 kilometres from us. This meant that he had to board at the school and was only able to come home during the school holidays. As our business often meant that we had to travel to that city, we were able to visit him during the school term.

When we made the *fenjia*, Zhen had become my responsibility. So when Cheng died in 1997, Zhen came to live with us in Wenxing. However, as we already had a nanny and a cleaner, Zhen quickly felt that there was little for her to do; she didn't feel needed and knew no one in the city. We also had little free time to be with her. After three months, Zhen decided to go back to Jin'e and live with Chun and Lan. I was sorry not to be able to fulfil my family responsibilities, but it was more important that Zhen is happy in her remaining years.

Nowadays, farmers do not need to pay any agricultural tax and the State pays subsidies for grain directly to farmers. They are now able to plant their fields with mechanization and can easily sell their crops. Conditions are now entirely different from when I started working with Zhen in the fields so many years ago. The memories of the days when we struggled to grow enough food are now receding. However, I still like to eat sweet potato every week, and I continue with my business. Our first son has studied at a good university overseas, and my second son is studying at a boarding school. When they stay with me, I like to cook them sweet potatoes.

Notes

1. Yuan Longping (2007) *What is hybrid rice: Yuan Longping Oral Autobiography* (Chinese Edition), Hunan Education Press.
2. *Gongliang* is the agricultural tax paid in grain.
3. Shang dynasty is generally dated from c. 1600 to 1046 BC. During this time, money was introduced into the economy and a tax system imposed on the population.

CHAPTER 8

Kai's Story: Fourth Daughter

When I look back on my childhood, I especially liked the rainy days when you could hear rain splattering on the roof and everyone was sheltering indoors. The house was full of people and noise, and neither Mu nor Baba went out to work. When Baba was in the house, I always felt safe and secure. He was so good at thinking of things to do. At the Spring Festival, Baba would make special snacks from sweet potato, corn, and brown sugar. Every year, he had new ideas as to how we would celebrate the festival. However, after I married, I found my husband's family didn't bother so much about celebrating the festival. I made some suggestions as to how we could make the festival into a happy family time. At first, the others weren't interested, but I persisted and slowly some of Baba's ideas became part of the life of my new family.

* * *

I was born in 1972 when my older sisters were 19, 17, and 15, and my brothers, Chun and Xia, were 11 and 5. As you can see, I grew up in a house full of people and noise, especially when Mu later had two more sons, Qiu and Dong. Mu was always strict and made sure that all of us children had jobs to do around the house; we weren't allowed to play unless we had done all our jobs well. Now that I am a mother, I can see that with eight children to look after and all the farm work to do, this was the only way that our family could prosper. Through this, we all learned the importance of hard work—an important lesson for us when we became adults.

Mu believed that women should look after men, and she required me to do the same. I know that in olden times, Chinese women used to do this, but we are now in a new era and we are taught that men and women are equal. However, when I was a child, this meant that I was responsible for washing my younger brothers' clothes, which included their underwear! Our house on Old Street was quite small, and with eight children, we didn't have much room, so I had to share a bed with Qiu and Dong. In the winter, Mu would send me to bed first so that I would warm the bed for the boys! Mu was insistent that all of us, boys and girls, had to get up to do 30–40 minutes of reading. We would sit at the gate of the house and read out loud. Qiu and Dong came and joined us when they became old enough. Although Mu couldn't read herself, she could hear us reading, so every school morning, our house was full of that sound. After this, we had our morning duties to do. My duty was to pick up any dog poo on the road in the neighbourhood and put it in the cesspit with the pigs' poo to make fertilizer for the fields. Ugh!

Because my three sisters were much older than me, I effectively grew up with my younger brothers. I can tell you that was hard! For example, I liked to get my housework done quickly so that I could have some time to play, but Qiu and Dong were always slow. Mu wouldn't let me go until all the jobs were done, and so I was always waiting for the boys to finish their duties. Another thing that annoyed me was that when I got some sweets from my sisters or neighbours, I would keep some for later, but if I left them about, my brothers would eat them. What is more, every time I complained to Mu, she would not stop them or punish them but would tell me to be more careful next time. I thought that was really unfair.

Because I was one year older than Qiu and three years older than Dong, Mu required me to look after them. Then, because Shun and her husband were busy, they asked for help in looking after their baby, so Mu and Baba insisted that he came to live with us in Jin'e. It then became my responsibility to look after all three boys! At that time, I was seven and they were six, four, and two! You can imagine how difficult it was to look after three naughty boys. They would sometimes band together to trick me and were always noisy; no wonder I got angry with them. Then, when I complained to Mu, she only said that as a girl, I should accept this sort of thing. I was disappointed that nobody supported me.

Every month, the commune would show a movie in the playground. As this was just outside our house, we kids would like to sit and watch the movie in the evenings. After dinner, we carried out benches to sit on, and when sufficient people had arrived, the movie would start. The movies were usually about the Japanese invasion of China or the civil war. I must admit that I wasn't particularly interested in them, but at that time movies were a great novelty for a little village like ours. Before the movie, I would always ask Dong and Jiang—Shun's son—if they needed to go to the toilet, and they would say no. Then, in the middle of the film, Dong or Jiang would wet their pants! When I took the boys home, Mu would blame me for their wet pants, which I then had to wash!

I liked to play with the other children, but with Mu, it was always work, work, and more work. I remember one day I arrived home from school, and Mu was not there, so instead of doing my jobs, I played in the playground with the other children. What I didn't know was that although Mu was far away in the fields, she could see me playing, and when she returned home, I was in trouble!

Some of my happiest times were when I was in primary school, when I was between the ages of 7 and 13. At break time, I could play with the other children without Mu calling me to do jobs. You can understand therefore why I didn't like weekends or holidays, as they just meant work. At school at least I could play some of the time. When I returned home from school, my first job was to get food for the pigs for the following day, which meant that I had to walk to the nearby hills with some of the other girls of the village. I had a big woven basket that I carried on my back. I was only small, and I couldn't gather all the food necessary for the pigs. Many times, when I returned home, my basket was not fully loaded, and Mu would scold me: "Why have you cut so little?" My friend later told me that as I walked back home, the movement would shake the foodstuff, so it settled lower in the basket. So as I got nearer home, I would take off the basket and bulk up the foodstuff to make the basket look full when I arrived home. I now realized that as an experienced farmer, Mu must have known about this trick, but she didn't criticize me and never commented on this again. I know that other members of my family thought of me as always complaining. Xia however was so different from me. He always seemed to be in a good mood and did his work without complaining. He even liked to sing while he did his homework or housework. I suppose that in every family there are different personalities.

My oldest brother-in-law, Ze, worked in the cooperative shop. In the 1970s, this was a good job because many products like salt and kerosene were rationed and were only sold by the cooperatives. When government policy changed, Ze was able to open his own store in the village. Sometimes he would bring his new stock back to our house to unpack, and this often included sweets. When there were no adults in the house, we kids would each take one of the sweets. We would only take one so that he didn't notice, but on one occasion, we all took two sweets! Ze realized what had happened, and we all got into trouble.

Baba took care of us girls, and I knew how much he loved me. I suppose that it was because I was much younger than my sisters. He often came home from work late in the evening, but I would like to wait for him so I could sit with him and eat some more food. However, Mu would often tell us to go straight to bed after we had finished our jobs in the evening.

After work Baba liked to play cards. He enjoyed this, and it let him build good relations with our neighbours. But Mu thought that he should be working and not playing cards. If Baba lost any money, Mu got angry with him, and if he'd also been drinking, they would argue and even hit each other. In his anger, Baba would often smash something. In the morning, they wouldn't speak to each other, and we kids would quietly get on with our jobs before going to school. Baba would fix what he had broken. By the time we returned home, Baba and Mu were usually speaking to each other again. I never liked the times they argued.

Another matter Baba and Mu sometimes disagreed about was that Baba wanted to try and find his younger brother. His mother had always wanted to know what happened to the child she abandoned all those years ago, and Baba felt this was an expression of his filial piety to her and his father. Mu didn't agree because she was worried that if Baba found him and he was poor, he would be another person for the family to feed. Baba always felt guilty that he never found out what happened to his younger brother.

As I said before, school holidays for me meant work, but National Children's Day was an exception. This is held every year on the first of June and is a holiday from primary school across the whole country. Often, the school organized a two-hour performance in the morning, when each class would present an act and teachers would also dance and sing with us. After the performance, the school gave us sweets and biscuits. On that day Mu didn't ask me to work, so I could go out and play all day with the other children. As my eldest sister, Shun also had much of the day free she would come to visit us. I knew that she was a qualified teacher, and so I had mixed feelings when she came to our home. On one hand, Mu would prepare special food, which was great, but on the other hand, Shun would always ask about my studies. Even though she was kind, I didn't like talking about my schoolwork, as I knew I was not a good student. I didn't realize until much later how much Shun was supporting the family at this time. She knew the important principle that family members must help each other, especially during difficult times.

The person I really loved was my second eldest sister, Shi. She was a tailor and made clothes for us. I remember she made my first set of new clothes. When she got married, the family had a wedding that followed the five traditional stages and took a long time to complete. The timing of the wedding was delayed because Mu didn't want Shi to leave the family home, as there was so much work to do looking after the younger children. However, in 1983, Shi left with her husband Hou for his home village of Guangming, but before she left, we all had a big party. Although I was excited about the party, I was sad that Shi would no longer be living with us. I must have been 11 or 12 at the time.

During Dragon Boat Festival and Moon Festival, both Shun and Shi would come home. I was pleased because they brought gifts of sweets and clothes. Baba also made traditional festival food like special dumplings. On her first few visits, Shi would tell me about her life after marriage and what she was doing. As a teenage girl, I think that it was Shi who gave me hope for my life in the future. Nevertheless, I remember she often cried because she was sad about the arguments she had with her husband, Hou. On one occasion, I remember she came home with a pole over her shoulder with her son in a basket at one end and unfinished garments at the other. The next day, Baba went to see Hou and told him that he should treat her better. Shi later returned home, once again carrying her son and the garments.

By that time, the economic conditions in the country were much better than in previous years, so I was fortunate to be able to go to junior high school in the county city where I boarded. I remember it was during those years that my third sister, Hua, argued with Mu and Baba. I didn't know much about it, but this had to do with a dispute about the piece of land she had tricked Baba over. It was a sad situation for the whole family.

When I failed the entrance examination for senior high school, I came back home to help with the work around the house and fields. Many things needed to be done, which kept me busy every day. With the improving economy, farmers were able to save a little money and some began to rebuild their houses. My family was able to build a new house after we sold dozens of pigs that Chun had given us to rear. We built our house near the town centre. So as to reduce costs, we did a lot of the work ourselves in addition to working in the fields. During the busiest days in the harvest month, we invited ten people from our clan to help us. They didn't charge us any money, but it was an unwritten agreement that when they needed help in the future, we would assist them. This is called *huan gong*, "exchange labour". Apart from helping with my brothers working on the building and farming, I was responsible for washing everyone's clothes. We had no washing machine and no water in the house, so you can imagine how hard I had to work. I had to carry all the clothes to a well half-an-hour's walk away, wash them by hand, and then carry them all the way back home. I also helped prepare the food for the pigs.

When the house was finished, my oldest brother-in-law, Ze, helped us open a grocery shop, and it became my responsibility to look after it. At first, I was often confused by the different products and how to keep the accounts and felt this was too much responsibility for somebody my age. At this time, the family had seven members living at home, and it seemed as though I lived surrounded by men who did not understand, and a mother who didn't have the time or patience to listen to me. I was so sad during this time! Then, my eldest brother, Chun, married and his wife, Lan, came to live with us. Lan's coming broke the stiff atmosphere of the family. She was soft and kind to all of us. She cared about all the brothers and sisters and was willing to listen to my complaints. I appreciated being able to talk to her about how I felt as a young woman.

Living with a different family was also difficult for Lan, as it was for most young brides. My parents, for example, believed in many superstitions, especially about the first day of the New Year. On that day, we couldn't open the front door because Baba and Mu thought it would invite trouble to enter the house. We couldn't use the words "*Guang*"(光), "*Tu*"(秃), or "*Mei you!*"(没有), which mean "empty" and "nothing", as they would imply we would have little income in the coming year. On the first day of the New Year, Lan got up early and opened the door as usual; Mu quickly ran and shut the door. When Lan asked why she had done this, I motioned to her to be quiet. Later, I heard Lan say to my brother "Don't *chiguang* all the rice balls"; *chiguang* means eat up. Mu quickly said, "We have lots of rice balls, enough to eat the whole year."

Poor Lan was very confused until I explained things to her later. Thereafter, Lan kept quiet or spoke only softly on the first day of New Year.

Even though I was responsible for looking after the store, Mu thought that I should still learn a trade. She didn't think that I was strong enough to be a farmer, so she encouraged me to study tailoring with Lan. I did try, but I was not good at tailoring. I had however kept contact with my classmates who were then working in the city and so I went to visit them. The city was so big and with so much to see. They encouraged me to leave our small village and join them in the city. I tried to find an opportunity to go and work in the city, but I had no contacts. Then, one of Shun's friends asked her if she knew of a nanny who could come and look after her child. To be honest, this was not the sort of job I would have chosen, but it looked like this was the only chance I could find to work in the city. So, I left home to start my first job.

The mother was an official and her husband was a county leader, and they always had friends visiting at weekends. I helped with looking after their two children and cooked for the family. At first, it was a real challenge for me, but I tried my very best. I saw how the lady had a good relationship with her husband and also their friends, and began to understand how important the role of the wife is in both family and work. After two years, the family moved to another city, but they helped me find an administrative job in the Agro-technical station in my hometown. There were six workers in the Agro-technical station, but I was the only one who hadn't graduated from college and didn't have a permanent contract. I worked hard and participated in self-study examinations, which I hoped would eventually give me a higher education degree. I also got some professional training in advanced plant skills. The station aimed to improve the skills of farmers by providing seed. I liked talking with different people and helping them with their particular situations. Now I was earning money, I was able to buy clothes for my two younger brothers. I wanted them to dress nicely, as I remembered how poor we had been as children. I also bought a lady's bike at a time when there were few in our town, and I would ride my bike to work every day.

At this time, fashionable clothes were becoming popular among young women, especially jeans, fitted pants, and tank tops. I bought some modern style of clothes for myself and even had my hair curled. In my family, all my sisters and sisters-in-law had short hair, so Mu was angry when I had my hair in curls. She said I was crazy and wanted to cut my hair, and we argued. I was now a young woman, and I thought that I should be allowed to look nice. I was so relieved when Lan intervened. She told Mu that this style was popular in the city, and it made me look beautiful. Mu trusted Lan so she stopped criticizing me for what I wore.

In February of 1997, Deng Xiaoping passed away. I still remember how sad we were on hearing this news. Deng had brought about many good reforms and was well liked by all the farmers. Baba went out into our yard and burnt several joss sticks for him. Then, on the first of July, there was a great handover ceremony of Hong Kong between the British government and the Chinese government under the constitutional principle of "One Country, Two Systems". On that day, all the TV stations broadcast the ceremony and many families sat watching the event. I remember the happiness of my colleagues and friends about this handover. This had been planned by Deng, as he wanted to reunite Hong Kong and Macau to the Motherland. He wisely proposed that after the Chinese government took them back, both areas would be allowed to continue to have their own governance style, including relations with foreign countries. We all thought that this was a good idea that would help unite our nation.

That same year, I had the chance to go to agricultural college for three years. Chun and Xia supported me, and I took some part-time jobs during my holidays. I met a lot of different people and they helped widen my perspective on life. I could see China was developing and people were becoming wealthier. My time at college totally changed me. Then, Baba died, and instantly it felt as though I was homeless. There is an old Chinese saying, "No parents, no home!" My older brothers, Chun and Xia, were now married, and they lived with their wives. On the day of the funeral, I was so sad and didn't want to leave Baba's tomb. Baba had always quietly supported me. I knew he hoped I would find a husband soon, but whenever somebody went to talk to him about this, he would always say, "No hurry, let her take her time." Once Baba was gone, I felt as though I no longer had a place at home anymore.

By this time, I was 28 years old, and the family wondered whether I would ever get married. I knew that some people already called me a *daling nuqingnian*, similarly to *shengnu*, the leftover lady.[1] The family started looking in earnest for a suitable man who was about my age. Shun introduced me to a colleague of hers, but I didn't like him because he was too quiet; I refused him. Mu finally said that I was free to accept any man as long as he was a hard worker, a non-drinker, and a non-smoker. What they didn't know was that I had already met a man who worked in the same department as me, and we had fallen in love. After graduating, I had gone back to my previous job, but now in a permanent role. I went home and much to their surprise, I told them I wanted to get married.

Ming was an intelligent man and had his own opinions. He also came from a farming family and was the oldest son. Even though he was the same age as me, he looked more mature. My family was delighted and hoped that we would marry soon. However, Mu insisted that since Baba had died the previous year, I had to consult my oldest brother Chun. In China, there is a proverb saying, "The oldest brother is like father." Lan told me that they were both pleased that I wanted to marry but suggested that we should go through the formal procedures. I didn't want to do this and argued against it. Shun said it was necessary, as it would protect me in the future if Ming or his family mistreated me. She then came up with the compromise that all the steps be combined into one. Although I was still not happy with this, I accepted her suggestion.

So, a little later, Ming's family sent a matchmaker to visit Zhen to formally propose marriage. Zhen and my two sisters-in-law went to visit Ming's family and they set a date for the marriage. Ming's family gave them all a gift, as was the custom. Then, a problem arose concerning my dowry. Chun and Xia both felt that, as they had paid all my tuition fees at college, they shouldn't have to contribute to the dowry. Lan, however, disagreed because she thought the brothers would lose face and I could easily be discriminated against by Ming's family in the future. She persuaded the brothers to contribute to the dowry, and they asked Lan to go with me to buy all the things I needed. My brothers then made equal payments for the dowry. I wanted to have everything for married life, including a television, refrigerator, washing machine, bedding, tables, chairs, basins, and bowls. By the end of our shopping, there were so many things that we had to ask Ming to send a truck to collect all the dowry goods.

After the wedding, I went to live with Ming and his family. Sadly, I found it uncomfortable living with them. Ming had a sister-in-law who didn't have a job and helped her parents-in-law with the farming. As a new daughter-in-law, I tried to be diligent and interested in the household like my sister-in-law, but it was difficult at first. I would sometimes go back to my home for some comfort from my family, but all they would say was that I should stop complaining. I knew that Ming's family respected me because I had a government job like Ming. Eventually, I was accepted into the family and grew to like all of them. A year after our marriage, in 2001, I had a daughter. Zhen was happy with the birth of the child, and Shun and her sister-in-law prepared many gifts to celebrate her birth. We named her Yuan. I had almost four months' maternity leave from my work and Ming's parents helped us to look after the baby until she was two years old, when we sent her to the nursery.

I continued to work hard and so sadly I had little time for Yuan. Five years later, I was promoted to the personnel department in Wenxing county, so Ming and I bought an apartment there. By this time, Yuan was old enough to go to primary school. My new job kept me very busy, and I often had to travel to different places in the county. Nevertheless, I still liked to keep in touch with all my family but they never seemed to appreciate how busy I was with my work and my responsibilities in Ming's household. As the oldest daughter-in-law in Ming's family, I took my responsibilities seriously and wanted to contribute to the life of the family. To my surprise, Ming got annoyed with me and told me that even though I had a lot of ideas, I should realize that other people have their own ideas and want to live their lives their own way. I protested, saying that I was only trying to help and show them a better way to do things.

Every Spring Festival, I went home to my family to spend some time with them, as is our custom. It is nice to eat and talk together. We liked to play mahjong, but I didn't like gambling and losing money. It is quite unfair, you know! They always win, just as they did when we were children. I liked to play for fun, but the others take the game seriously. As a result, my brothers prefer to play with Ming. Every time they want to play cards, they always ask, "Where's Ming?" even if I am standing right in front of them. Whenever this happens, Mu only smiles but says nothing.

In 2008, I was promoted again, this time to become the chair of the Countryside Women's Federation (CWF), which is responsible for maintaining women's rights in the whole of the county. In China, it acts as the official leader of the women's movement, and its main responsibility is to promote the government's policies about women and to protect women's rights. It was started in 1949 at the beginning of the Chinese Communist Party (CCP) government. The CWF has long been supported by the CCP so most people tend to see it as part of the Party. I am not a member of the Communist Party but represent one of the smaller, alternative parties.

One of the Federation's major tasks is to try and improve the quality of life for women and their employment opportunities. We arrange a variety of training programmes which address different social themes: "How to get along with your mother-in-law and sister-in-law" and "How to work as a nanny." You can see that these are really practical courses that can help women find jobs and improve their family life. I have participated in many exciting training courses sponsored by the Provincial Federation and Prefectural Federation. After each of them, I share what I have learned with my colleagues. We spent a lot of time visiting more than 20 of the poorest villages near our town. We sometimes stay in the villages and listen to the women's stories. Many of their husbands work as labourers in big cities like Shanghai and Guangzhou. We support them to ensure that their rights are recognized, especially when they have problems with an abusive husband. We provide employment information and organize workshops about new employment opportunities such as poultry farming and making handicraft items.

Wherever I go, I always encourage the girls to keep studying at school rather than going to the big city as a migrant worker when they are still young. I tell their parents that going to school is the best way for their daughter to fulfil her destiny. We have helped many girls to apply for loans and grants to continue at school. Ever since 2012, jobs for women have been emphasized by the government. There is now a "Ladies Loans" system that allows a woman to borrow interest-free up to 80,000 RMB from the government to start their own business. Of course, we also help them with business planning. I am often moved by their subsequent success and happiness.

I am also deputy head of the Conciliation Centre of Marriage and Family Disputes and an Assessor at Court. I talk with visitors and listen to the conflicts in their marriages. I carefully ask each woman about her hopes, and try my best to act appropriately in terms of their various appeals. I later revisit them and ensure they are fine. Sadly in the countryside, there have been many left-behind women, and in my role as an assessor, I actively invite some staff and volunteers from the judicial department to give lectures as to how they can exercise their legal rights. We try to improve their legal knowledge, reduce the possibility of infringement, and at the same time prevent crime.

Another activity I am involved with is the "Looking for the most Beautiful Family", a campaign launched by the National Ladies Federation to promote traditional family values. This enables us to help some families in many different ways. For example, in May 2016, two children were orphaned when their father died on the first day of the month. One child was aged eight and the other was five. We informed the local government, who paid for the funeral and contributed an additional 120,000 RMB to support the children until they reach adulthood. Two families wanted to adopt the children, but this would have meant that the children would be separated at this critical time in their life. Fortunately, we managed to find their grandparents, and the children preferred to go and live with them. This was a happy ending to what was a sad story. In another case, there was a 40-year-old lady, whose husband was arrested for some offence. She was unable to support herself and her nine-year-old daughter. The Ladies Association was able to give her some money, help her to receive counselling, and participate in a skills training course so that she could find a job to support the two of them.

Another activity of the Ladies Association is encouraging women between 30 and 60 to have regular check-ups for the two main forms of women's cancer—breast and cervical cancer. In all villages, the check-up is now free of charge. We have also made an arrangement with an Insurance Company to offer a policy for 100 RMB that provides treatment free of charge if the cancer recurs within the following ten years. This has become very popular with many women.

One of our most important projects relates to those who are called "left-behind children". These are children whose parents have moved to the cities to find work and are being looked after by their grandparents in the countryside. The problems are not just about food and clothing, but these children don't get enough love and lack a sense of security. Their parents only come home for a couple of weeks each year at Spring Festival and are gone again. Their grandparents either spoil them or discipline them too much. This causes them some major psychological problems.

In 2016, it was decreed that each village should have a programme called "Love Family for Left Behind Children". Local schools are responsible for this, and each village appoints a ladies official who should also be a member of the village committee. Each village should have a Ladies Committee. These days, the government is paying a lot of attention to training for girls, to the extent that many parents now hope to have a girl because girls have a lot of social advantages.

I started a new NGO in Wenxing county that works with left-behind children; it's called "Smell of Roses". I am so pleased that our volunteers come from every level of society. They try to find a substitute mum for each child. Each summer, several hundred children are chosen to participate in the campaign, and special events are arranged with the local schools. Although our power is limited, we try our best to provide support for these children.

Though my work with the Ladies Association keeps me busy, I find it extremely satisfying, as I am able to help a lot of people. I remember when I was a girl, how I had to look after my younger brothers and wash their clothes. I knew that my parents loved me, but in those days, it was the custom for boys to be seen as being of more worth than girls; now we are in a new age. I want women and girls to have equal opportunities to those of men and boys.

In 2016, I was recommended to become one of the 13 members of the CPPCC[2] representing Wenxing for the prefectural district. This is a five-year position. Every year, about 200 members of the CPPCC gather for the annual meeting. As a CPPCC member, I have the right to propose suggestions involving the daily life of ordinary people. These suggestions then go to the appropriate department, which must provide a response. I have made suggestions concerning left-behind children and ladies' rights in cases of divorce. I am pleased that I can help to make a difference.

Ming has kept at his studies during the years we have been married and has recently been promoted to manager in one of the key government departments in the county. My daughter is now studying at high school, but she is not as good a scholar as I would have wished. I will try my best to support her and create good conditions for her. Whatever she wants to study, I encourage her to try. Unlike my childhood and teenage years, she has the chance to choose from many things in her future. I also try to pay more attention to her puberty and psychological health. The role of women has changed a lot, even in my own lifetime. I think a young woman today should be happy and optimistic as she grows up in new China.

When I was young, Mu would sometimes beat me if I was lazy, and I was not allowed to talk back to my parents or I would be in even bigger trouble. One time, I got angry and had the same attitude towards my own daughter, but she immediately responded, "You do not have the right to hit me, I am an independent person." I was shocked and then realized that the younger generation is much more confident and self-assured than mine ever was. Then I realized that this is actually the goal of my work.

The conditions for my daughter are so much better than those I had. As she has never needed to look after her brothers or sisters as part of her daily life, she has been able to study piano, dance, and drawing. I used to think that she should pay all her attention to her academic work, and so I did everything that I could do to help her concentrate on this. Now, I realize that this was a mistake, and she should be able to choose for herself. Academic study is only one aspect of one's life.

NOTES

1. In terms of "The China Language Situation Report (2006)", released by the Ministry of Education in 2007, this is one of the 171 new words in Chinese. It refers to a woman who is generally considered over marriageable age.
2. The Chinese People's Political Consultative Conference (CPPCC) is one of the important organizations of the Chinese political situation. At the Conference, the Communist Party of China (CCP) has about two-thirds of the seats. Other members are drawn from the United Front parties allied with the (CCP) and from independent members who are not members of any Party. The Conference is intended to be more representative and be composed of a broader range of people than is typical of a government office in the People's Republic of China.

CHAPTER 9

Qiu's Story: Third Son

In 1973, Zhen gave birth to her seventh child, her third son. That was me—Qiu. I had two brothers and three sisters who were much older than me, so my life was mainly centred around my sister Kai, who was one year older, and my brother Dong, who was two years younger. I remember how Kai was put in charge of me and Dong, but although she did her best, we were often naughty. Dong and I used to have some great times together, but Mu was very strict. As there were many children in the family, she insisted that even the youngest of us children had to do some housework or she would punish us. Dong and I thought that housework was really boring and we didn't like doing it, and so we would only do it reluctantly. Kai did her work quickly and then told us to hurry up so she could go out and play. We didn't listen to what she said because we knew that Mu favoured us boys over the girls.

When I was eight, I became a student at the local primary school. Shi, my second eldest sister, by that time had left school, and in the evenings, she tried to help us with our homework. I remember her telling us of what it had been like when she went to school, and how she wanted us to be dressed nicely. I must admit that I was not an outstanding student, and my parents were concerned as to whether I would be able to pass the junior high school Student Recruitment Examination. At this time, only primary education was compulsory and less than half the children from our village went on to study at the junior high school.

One day, after once again coming at the bottom of the third grade, Mu shouted at me, saying that I was lazy and should get out of the house. I ran out of the door and went to hide in the fields behind the house; I hoped that Mu would soon come looking for me. But she didn't! When night came and the wind blew cold, I huddled in a sheltered corner, scared because of the snakes that lived in the fields and the mosquitos that buzzed around my ears. At one time, I crept up to the back of the house to see what they were doing and if they were worried about me. I was sad to find out that nobody seemed concerned about my absence. Mu didn't come looking for me, and she didn't even send one of my brothers or sisters to look for me. Two days later, I returned home hungry and tired, and, I admit, sad and disappointed that nobody seemed to care.

Later, because of my bad scores, the family decided to transfer me to the school where Shun taught, so she could supervise my studies. There I joined my younger brother Dong. Shun was strict like Mu, but she was kind and helped me with some extra tuition. After 2 years, when I was about 13, I did finally manage to pass the examination and went on to junior high school in Jin'e. The school had only just been built, and I was one of the first students to study there. While I was in the first year of junior high school, the county established a new boarding school in the county town and appointed some of the best teachers from the county to teach there. In order to study at the boarding school, students needed to pay fees for their accommodation and food. Although our family was not rich, they always tried to take advantage of any new opportunities. They decided they could afford to pay for one child to study at boarding school but not two. They chose Dong! I must admit that I was very disappointed about this, but there was nothing I could do.

It was in 1990, whilst I was in the final year of junior high school, an event happened that would shape the rest of my life. One day, I saw two of my classmates fighting. I didn't like to see a weaker boy being picked on, and as I was tall and strong for my age, I went to separate them. I must admit that even now I can't stand injustice. I quickly separated them, but the bigger boy hit me, causing a gash on my face. The Head Class Teacher showed me no sympathy and said I shouldn't get involved in this sort of thing. My parents were asked to go to the school, and Mu took me to the hospital and had to pay for the medical expenses. Shun scolded me saying that I must have offended the boy; otherwise, I wouldn't have got into such a situation. I thought that this was really unfair, and I was so upset about my family's misunderstanding. The boy who hit me came from the Wang family, the clan that Mu came from. This family had an ongoing grudge against my father because he had seen one of the Wang family stealing something from one of our neighbours. When the neighbour came asking for information, Baba told him what he had seen. Later, this family had a disagreement with my oldest uncle, my mom's brother. Ever since then, our families have been in conflict. Well, when the boy returned home after the fight, he told his parents that because I had stopped him, he was not able to hit back at the other classmate. One day, when I was passing their house, his dad stopped me, smacked me, and warned me to leave his son alone.

I didn't like the boy because the teachers were always saying how good his scores were and how poor mine were. I was hurt by the criticism from both the school and my family, but there was nothing I could do, so I remained silent. My marks declined, and I didn't want to go to school anymore. To make things worse, the Wang family lived close to the school, next to the Agro-technical centre, where my sister Kai worked. The mother of the Wang boy often abused Kai and made life difficult for her. I decided that I would wait for a suitable time when I could get my own back on him. Then, one day, Yi and another classmate who also had a disagreement with him proposed that we beat him up. So I agreed!

This was the time of year when examinations were held to select students who would go on from junior high school to a vocational college. Students who pass the exam got a full scholarship for their studies and were guaranteed a job in a local government department. For students from a peasant background like us, this was an important achievement, but the competition was so great that in our area only about 5% passed the exam. If you didn't pass, the only option was to continue at senior high school and face the challenges of the *gaokao* examination when you were about 19. This would mean that the family would then have to support their child for at least three more years at school and longer if they went on to university. All the teachers thought that the Wang boy would get a good score and pass the exam.

We waited for the day of the exam. But on that morning, Baba asked me to clean the pigsty, which made me late getting to school. However, Yi and the other classmate attacked the Wang boy and beat him up. They ran away laughing leaving him on the ground, cut and bruised. When I arrived, they told me what had happened. Although I apologized for being late, I could see they were unhappy with me. The boy did badly in the exam and failed. The day after the examination, his family took things into their own hands. They went to Yi to find out about the assault and said if he told them whose idea it was, they would not report him to the police. Yi said that all the ideas had come from me, so the Wang family called on some of their clan members to beat me up.

Since they thought I wouldn't be staying in our house, they went to the houses of all my married sisters where they thought I might be hiding. When the gang came and knocked on Shun's door, it was Ze who answered. He was puzzled as to what was going on and why they were looking for me. After they had left, Shun immediately rushed to our house. It was a lazy summer afternoon, and I was taking a nap. She told me what had just happened, and I told her the whole story. She told me to go quickly and hide somewhere. The gang continued to search for me for three days while I remained in the outhouse of one of Shun's friends, frightened and alone. Shun reported the matter to the local police but didn't realize that the head of police was a friend of the Wang family and so didn't take the matter seriously. The Wang family kept looking for me, and it became clear that they weren't about to give up. Shun decided that I had to leave the village and go away to a city to avoid the conflict; otherwise, there would be no peace for the family. The night before I left, I was in the house of my second sister, Shi. I still remember that night; it was pouring with rain. Baba came to Shi's house to see me. He was 70 years old and had just been diagnosed with tuberculosis. He gave me all the money he had in his pocket and said that I had to look after myself. Finally, he told me not to do anything illegal. My eyes were full of tears! I think that it was only then that I realized the old truth that when you are in extreme difficulties, it is only your parents who really care about you.

As darkness fell the following day, I slipped out of the village with a small bag of clothes over my shoulder. I walked all through the night and the whole of the next day to the capital town of the neighbouring county where I could catch a bus to Wuhan. This was the only way I could get away without being spotted, as the gang were watching the local bus station. I was so tired by the time I reached the town, I could barely stand. I had never been so far away from home before. When I left, I was 18; I have never returned to Jin'e.

I went to Wuhan because Shun knew two farmers from the village where she taught who were working there. She didn't actually know what they did, but she arranged for me to join them. I had never been to a big city before, and I was confused by all the streets and traffic. I was so relieved to finally meet up with the two farmers and happy to sleep in their rough shelter. It was on the first night I went out to work with them that I suddenly realized what they were doing; they were stealing materials from construction sites. There I was helping them; I was terrified of getting caught. After a week, I was more familiar with the surroundings and started looking for a regular job. I soon found one as a labourer at a building site.

Many farmers found work on such construction sites because the jobs required few skills, only brute strength to carry the heavy loads. The work was hard and the hours were long; we worked every day from dawn to dusk. We slept in the sheds on the construction site, and every night, I fell asleep to the sound of migrant workers' snoring. I couldn't go back home, but what sort of life was this? I couldn't tell my family what had happened to me although I knew they would be worried. Day in, day out, I laboured harder than I had ever done in my life. I looked at the new apartments we were building and wished that one day I could live in such a place rather than on a dusty, noisy construction site.

Occasionally, I met up with a friend I knew from Jin'e. When he returned home, he told Shun about what I was doing in Wuhan, and she was concerned for me. She then remembered that a relative of the clan of Baba's stepfather was working in Chengdu, the capital of Sichuan Province. So she arranged for me to go from Wuhan to Chengdu. Through the help of this relative, whose name was Ding, I found a job as a security guard in a company that manufactured gas appliances. This was a much better job than the one I had in Wuhan, and I worked there for several years.

When I was 22, I met a girl at Ding's house. Her name was Ju. She also came from Jin'e and was about the same age as me. She and I were actually distant members of the same clan on my mother's side. We quickly became friends. Ju told me how she had moved from Jin'e when she was 16 and went to work for her cousin in Chaoyang. When she left home, Ju was excited about the future, as this was her first time to go to a big city. Once she arrived in Chaoyang, she was overwhelmed by all the people and cars and felt confused and lost. She worked as a nanny for her cousin's children, but this was not easy, as she didn't understand city life and often made mistakes. She worked hard all day and sometimes cried at night. She only went back to Jin'e once during that time, which was for the two-week holiday at the Spring Festival. When she was at home, she didn't want to return to the city but realized this was the best opportunity she could have. If she stayed in Jin'e, matchmakers would soon come to propose marriage for her to some man. Once married, she would soon have children and then never leave the village. This was not the life she hoped for. Ju therefore went back to Chaoyang and gradually overcame her fears.

When she was 18, her cousin and family moved to Chengdu in order to develop their business and Ju moved with them. Ju liked Chengdu and started thinking about having her own business. She didn't know how to do this, but as her cousin's business expanded, she was given added responsibilities. She not only looked after the two children but was also involved in some aspects of the business. Her cousin even paid for her to go to driving school, so she could drive the children to their various activities. Ju gained confidence and began enjoying life in the city. With her new responsibilities, she was earning 300 RMB per month, more than she had ever had before. She was now able to buy gifts for her family in Jin'e. When she returned home for the Spring Festival, she brought with her a television, electric blanket, shoes, and clothes as gifts.

Ju was the first girl I had known apart from my sisters. When she told me her story, I was very moved. Then I told her my story, and we realized we had had similar difficult experiences. We came from the same village, same clan, and had both left home when young. I thought Ju was pretty and cute, and Ju thought that I was hard working and good looking. You might guess that our relationship quickly developed. As a security man, I was responsible for the flowers used to decorate the office, and every evening, I would tidy up the old flowers. I would sort out the best and take a bundle of them as a gift for Ju. We would meet each other outside her cousin's house and would walk together for half an hour or so along the city streets. I was Ju's first boyfriend. You can imagine how happy we both were.

However, Ju's cousin didn't think that I was a suitable husband for Ju. She told Ju that as she had now left the village, she could find a man who had a better financial and social status than me. Ju replied that she loved me and argued that even if I was a beggar, she would go to beg with me. When her cousin realized Ju's determination, she thought the only way to help her was to improve my position. As a result, she found a better job for me, working as a salesman at her husband's company in Guangzhou, where she hoped I would be able to study sales and marketing. This job had a salary three times that of my job as a security officer. So, I left Ju and went to work in Guangzhou, but I didn't get on well with my colleagues and my boss wasn't pleased with my work. He exaggerated my poor performance, so Ju's cousin once again objected to our hopes of getting married. After six months, I returned to Chengdu, and in spite of the fact that her cousin disagreed, Ju left her cousin's house and came to live with me. We used our limited savings to set up our own home in a rented apartment. This was 1996, and I was 24.

I soon found a job, this time with Ding's husband who was a butcher. Although the work was hard, I quickly learned the skills, and after three months, I started working independently. The nature of the work meant that I had to leave home around two o'clock in the morning, go and buy two or three pigs, and then wait for them to be slaughtered. I used to lean against the wall and fall asleep as the pigs squealed at the other end of the slaughterhouse. Once the pigs were slaughtered, I would take them to the market and cut them up to sell. I would arrive at the market at about 5 a.m. and Ju would come and join me at 7 a.m., so we worked together until afternoon by which time most of the meat was sold. I then went back home to sleep and Ju finished all the business by dinner time. Like all of us who grew up in a poor village, we had two assets: we were able to work hard and to endure suffering. We worked like this seven days a week. After deducting the rent and daily costs, we had little surplus but we were still full of hope and we were happy together.

Most migrants return home at the Spring Festival, but for the first three years, I didn't want to go back home. This was because it allowed me to earn some extra money and also save on travelling expenses. During the two weeks of the holiday, the city was cold and empty as thousands of migrant workers left for their homes. We therefore invited migrant friends who were staying in the city to join us for a meal and we then watched the Spring Festival Gala on CCTV and enjoyed the firework display. On the following days, we visited the homes of other friends in the city. The children were wrapped up in their coats watching TV, with no demands for them to do homework. The men played mahjong without women interfering. The wives chatted, cooked food, cracked sunflower seeds, and either complained or boasted about their husbands. For us, this was the most relaxed time during the whole year, but we still missed our families back in the village.

I still remember the first Spring Festival that we returned to Wenxing. We first had to take a 12-hour train journey and then transfer to a bus. We knew the train would be crowded, but we had never seen anything like this before! Boarding the train, people were carrying sacks on their shoulders, shouting to each other as they squeezed into the carriages. Many people couldn't get in through the doors so they climbed in through the windows. All the seats were full, people were standing in the passageways, and even the toilets were crowded. Everyone had only one idea in mind, which was to get onto the train to go home. People had brought instant noodles to eat, heavy bags full of gifts for the family, and some even carried a small stool. After 50 weeks of working hard in the city, we were all heading home!

The flow of students and migrant workers mixed together in the crush for the train. During the long journey, people chatted with each other, sharing their experiences of working in the city and talking about the money they had saved. They also talked about their personal lives. Many had not seen their children since the previous Spring Festival and were wondering how they had got on being looked after by grandparents. Some had not seen their husband or wife for many months, as they worked in a different city. Twenty years ago, people didn't have smartphones and there were no high-speed trains, so it was difficult to keep in contact with families and friends.[1]

I remember one time going to buy tickets at the station. I arrived at 7 a.m. on a bitterly cold morning and was surprised at the long queue that had already formed. Some people tried to push into the queue, but they were always stopped and shouted at that they should go to the back. Some people wore only thin coats and were jumping up and down on the spot to get warm. It was boring just standing there, so I started talking with the lady ahead of me. She told me how much she missed her two children who lived back in her home village. She and her husband had worked in Chengdu for three years and this was the first time they were able to go back home to celebrate the Spring Festival. So many times, she had dreamed of her children, and she was so excited that she would soon see them again. After two hours, she finally got to the ticket desk and as she was getting her money out, the desk closed, as the tickets were all sold out. The lady burst into tears and sobbed uncontrollably. The ticket seller looked with sympathy, but there was nothing he could do. She had to choose another train going later, and so had to join that queue. I never knew what happened to her that day.

When my economic situation improved, I was able to invite Baba and Mu to come and visit us in Chengdu, as I knew they would be pleased that Ju was pregnant. Although Baba was old and in poor health, he made the long journey by bus. For both of them, this was the first time they had come to a big city. Before they left, I told them to pack lightly; otherwise, their luggage would be a bother for them on the journey. When I found them at the bus station, there they were, each standing with two big bags. Baba and Mu both looked older and thinner. Mu's hair was white and Baba's skin was sallow and his eyes heavy. I couldn't stop my tears. It was six years since I had last seen them. I knew that even after I had left Jin'e, the Wang family had continued to make trouble for them. My brothers wanted to fight the Wang family, but Baba and Mu had stopped them. All their lives, they were cautious and tried to avoid conflicts with neighbours, but I had caused them big problems. I realized how hard it had been for them, as they took the pressure for me. I felt so sorry for them. When we arrived at our home, they opened their four big bags. One bag contained their clothing, and the other three were filled with all kinds of vegetables and foods from Jin'e, including my favourite green Chinese onions from their garden. I cried as I realized how much they actually loved me.

We had a good time together, and I took them to see many sights in the city. I wanted to take them to have meals in a restaurant, but they refused because Baba said it was too expensive and he could cook for us. Baba was always a good chef, and even though his health was not good, he liked to cook various local dishes. After two weeks, they went home. We said our goodbyes at the bus station. Both Baba and I realized that we would probably not see each other again. I remember seeing Baba's bony hand waving as the bus moved off on its long journey home. His hand had supported me in my youth, and now he was gone. Sadly, I turned and went back to my business. There is an old Chinese saying, "the saddest tragedy is that of the son who wants to serve his parents in their old age, but they are no more alive."

Baba's health soon deteriorated. Chun, my eldest brother, tried his best to support Baba and arranged for him to be treated by the best doctor in the region. This care helped Baba to live a little longer. Then, one morning, Baba got up and went to the toilet but suffered a cerebral haemorrhage. He was 73 when he died in Chun's house. Two weeks before he died, we were able to tell him the good news that Ju had given birth to twin boys.

Mu had always been strict in the way she brought us up, and I admire her for that because I now realize how difficult it was to feed so many children at that time. Nevertheless, when I look back, I feel that it was only my eldest sister, Shun, who really showed me much affection. In those hard times, Shun often acted as Mum to me, and it was because of her strength that the family now has a good life. Even today, I like to phone Shun whenever I feel sad, and we have good talks together. She was always very understanding.

At first, I had always found Ju caring and loving, but after the birth of the twins, she was always tired and preoccupied with the children. We were both working hard and so I guess that was the reason we started arguing. I found Ju would sometimes say stupid things, and I would get angry with her. When we argued, neither of us would compromise, and it left us both feeling upset and depressed. We were both struggling and didn't know how to deal with it. I talked to Shun about our situation, and she suggested that we needed to be more understanding of each other and talk about how we felt. But, sometimes any attempt at talking turned into an argument. Ju used to shout at me and say that now she saw me for who I really was. That hurt me!

When the twins were three years old, Ju went to talk with her cousin, saying that she couldn't stand this sort of life anymore and asked for her help. Her cousin was kind to her and listened to all she had to say. She then suggested that we needed to change our work, as we were both overtired. Ju and I decided to give up our jobs in Chengdu and go to Guangzhou. Like many other migrants, we sent the twins to live with family members in the countryside. The twins became left-behind children living with Chun and Lan in Jin'e. I have to say we were really lucky because Lan was patient and kind and loved our children like she loved her own. At this time, all my brothers and sisters were married and worked in Wenxing or a big city. Mu therefore moved in to live with Chun, and we sold our old house in Jin'e. This allowed Mu to help Lan to look after the twins.

Living in Guangzhou was different this time. Ju's cousin arranged for me to work at her husband's company selling cloth wholesale. I worked in the marketing department, supervised by a senior sales manager. She also arranged for Ju to join the logistics department. Both of us were grateful for this new opportunity, were careful to keep on good relations with our colleagues, and followed all the procedures of the company. After two years, we had gained a good knowledge of the business, and we left to start a company of our own.

In 2005, we registered our business in Guangzhou. We rented a store and warehouse, employed several workers, and started selling cloth wholesale to outlets in every province of the country. We benefitted from the growth in the market at that time, and the business went very well. After two years, we were able to buy an apartment and a car, so that the twins were able to come and live with us again. Nevertheless, as Ju and I were both busy, we didn't have much time to look after the boys. As Shun had retired from her primary school, we suggested that she come with the children so she could act as their tutor. Ze, her husband, also came with Shun and looked after the house. Things seemed to be working well, but Ju and I continued to quarrel. She complained that I didn't care about her, and I didn't think she was soft towards me anymore.

In 2007, we decided to explore the markets in the nearby province of Zhenjiang. We divided the work so that Ju was responsible for exploring markets in Guangzhou, whilst I went with another sales person to Zhenjiang.

Unfortunately, this meant that we were often living in different cities, so we had little time together. The other salesperson was kind and looked up to me. Slowly I became attracted to her, and she to me. You can guess what happened! When Ju heard about this, she was furious and wanted to separate.

After a year, I moved out of the house in Guangzhou and started my own business in Zhenjiang. There were great opportunities in the growing Chinese export market, and I put all my emphasis into this. Then, the global economic crisis came in 2008, and my overseas markets suddenly dried up. I was left with large quantities of unsold stock; my business collapsed and I was bankrupt. Ju's business, however, continued to do well as she still had good domestic markets. I returned back to Guangzhou and asked Ju to accept me back. She did, but life was never quite what it had been before, and we continued to argue. I think this was when I realized I no longer loved Ju and both of us decided it was time to divorce. That was in 2012. Soon after the divorce, I married the young woman who was 15 years my junior. My family were against this marriage because my new wife was so much younger than me, and they still considered Ju to be a member of the family. Nevertheless, I persisted and now have a happy marriage with her and our two children.

Many people felt that we shouldn't have divorced because we had a good business and a couple of healthy boys, but we decided that we couldn't continue living in that way. In order to lessen the negative impact of our arguments on the twins, we sent them to one of the best boarding schools in the province. The twins studied hard and spent the holidays, not in Guangzhou, but in Jin'e with Chun and Lan. All the members of Zhen's wider family loved the twins and supported them a lot. The boys often say they are not only the children of me and Ju but of Zhen's wider family. Because of their love for the boys, this has reduced the impact of the divorce, and both boys are doing well.

I have to say I am very proud of my twin boys. They both did well in the *gaokao* and received university offers. Being unable to go to university myself had been a big disappointment for me, but I am pleased that my sons now have the opportunity. One is studying artificial intelligence and the other is in medical school training to be a doctor. Wherever I see a book which I think would be useful for them, I always buy it and post it to them. I ask them to send me back their reading notes, but they sometimes complain it is too much work! I hope that in the future, I will be able to create a good financial situation for all members of my family. Perhaps this will be one way I can express my love for them.

Note

1. In 2016, 2.9 billion passenger journeys were undertaken by Chinese during the Spring Festival. The 40-day travel period around the Spring Festival is called *Chunyun*, meaning "national migration". Nowadays, train tickets can be booked by smartphone so people no longer have to queue in the cold weather to buy tickets. People can take high-speed trains, making travel much faster, but some people, in order to save money, still choose to take the slow trains. Although previously travellers brought lots of luggage with gifts for children, parents, and relatives, today, they buy gifts from the likes of Alibaba and Amazon and have them delivered directly to their home.

CHAPTER 10

Dong's Story: Fourth Son

I was the last of the eight children in our family, born in 1975, when Zhen was 43 and Cheng was 51. My oldest sister Shun was 22 then, and I only remember her and my other two older sisters as adults. The economic situation in the 1970s was much improved since Shun was a child. For me, knowledge of the changes they had lived through was only what I learnt from their daily conversation. As the proverb goes, "the emperor loves the eldest son and the common people love the youngest son". Perhaps it was because I was the youngest son that I was somewhat spoilt by my elder brothers and sisters. I grew up with Kai, Qiu, and my nephew Jiang. As Kai was the youngest daughter, she was appointed to look after the three of us boys. Poor Kai, we often caused her problems because we liked to play and sometimes we got into trouble.

One of my earliest memories relates to the pigsty. I don't remember much about what happened, but the family always liked to tell this story. In the countryside, many households have a pigsty, which is usually raised from the ground so that the pig shit falls through the bamboo floor into a pit below. Our toilet was next to the pigsty so that our shit would also fall into the same cesspit. The content of the cesspit was then spread on the fields as fertilizer. It was when I was about four years old and I was on my own, squatting beside the pigsty, watching the newly born piglets feeding from the sow. Suddenly, the sow kicked her foot as if she was going to stand up. I panicked and jumped up, but I fell backwards into the cesspit and sank into the shit pond. The pigsty was alongside the kitchen where Shi was preparing the pigs food.

She heard the sound and quickly rushed into the pigsty. She saw me struggling in the cesspit and quickly reached down, grabbed me, and pulled me out. I had swallowed a lot of the shit, but as we lived close to the village hospital, she quickly carried me there to have my stomach pumped out. I remember feeling unwell for many days afterwards. I would sit at the front door with a swollen stomach, feeling very sad for myself and not wanting to play with anyone. Mu and Baba said that when this sort of misfortune happens, the child must have rice from the homes of seven families with different names. Mu therefore went to different homes and asked each of them to give her a little rice so that I would get well. Today, we don't believe in this sort of thing—but eventually I did get better.

As I said, Shun's son, Jiang, was a little younger than me and came to live with us when he was six months old. We liked playing together. Baba would look after the two of us, and we enjoyed being with him. On market days, the villagers would often come to see Baba, as they knew he was a vet. They would come carrying their chicken or piglet for Baba's attention and wait in the concrete yard in the front of the house. Jiang and I would push chairs forward for the visitors and stand around watching Baba operate on the animals.

Baba sat by the door on a small stool. He would take hold of a cock, skilfully place it on its back, and hold its legs and wings to the floor with his feet. The bird would shriek in protest, but Baba's castrating knives, pliers, and disinfectant iodine were already at hand, and the operation was quickly done. Pigs are stronger than chickens so Baba needed the help of the farmer to hold them down, but once again the task was quickly accomplished. The farmers would pay Baba and leave with their animals still complaining at the way they had been treated.

By noon, the queue of farmers had gone, and Jiang and I collected the animal excrement, put it in the manure pit under the pigsty, and then washed the yard. We knew that after we finished these jobs, Baba would give us some money. We then hurried to the local store to buy a rice bun. Baba wanted us to show it to him first, and then we would sit in the yard, enjoying the bun. Sometimes, I ate most of the bun on the way back home, and all I had left to show Baba was a small portion of rice. Over the past years, I have eaten many tasty foods in different restaurants, but none of them has ever tasted as delicious as the little rice buns of my childhood.

When I was ten, I was made responsible for looking after the cattle. I would sit on a stone and read whilst the cattle grazed in the field, but one day, I was so enthralled in my book that I didn't notice that the cattle were escaping. When I realized what was happening, I quickly dashed to the gate, but the cows were already walking down the path. They scared an elderly neighbour when they pushed her aside, and she fell and hurt her leg. I herded the cattle back into the field and ran off to find Baba. Baba and Mu quickly came and helped the lady and took her to hospital where they paid the medical fees. Later, they brought some gifts for the lady, and they required me to apologize to her. I knelt before her and bowed, asking her to forgive me for not looking after the animals more carefully. The lady's son demanded that Baba pay some money as compensation, but the old lady protested. "Cheng's family were always hardworking and kind." She said, "They have many children and life has not been easy for them. Let us not overdo it because we live in the same village." I was very upset at what had happened and expected Baba and Mu to be angry with me, but they only warned me to be more careful in the future.

Later I was able to go on to junior high school where I continued to get good grades. Although our family wasn't rich, they decided they could afford to pay for one child to study at boarding school. They had to choose between Qiu and me; as my scores were always much higher than Qiu's, they chose me. I could see how disappointed Qiu was, but he always struggled with his studies whereas I enjoyed schoolwork.

In 1990, when I was 15, Qiu got into real trouble after an argument he had with a boy in his class. The situation was so bad that the only thing that the family could do was to send him away to find work in the city. Baba and Mu were both upset, and I was so sad for Qiu. One evening when it got dark, he quietly slipped away from the village and walked all the way to the next county. I had lived and played with Qiu all my life, and I really missed him. I didn't see Qiu again for several years.

When I began boarding at the city junior high school, I had much more freedom there than when I was living at home where there was endless housework. Now I could arrange my own time at the weekends, but surprisingly I soon became bored. I therefore invited other classmates to play cards. What I didn't know was that one of my teachers was a friend of Shun's, and she told her I was being naughty and not paying attention to my studies. Shun told her friend to treat me as if I was a brother and scold me if she thought that I was being lazy or doing anything wrong. After that, trouble came! This teacher started treating me just like Shun did, and whenever I made a mistake at school, she always gave me a hard time. I still remember the way she would look at me if I wasn't paying full attention to my studies.

I graduated from junior high school with top grades, sufficient to study at the teacher training college. This was still the goal of the top students in small towns like ours. However, there was only one place available for our town. There were only two candidates for the position, me and a girl who had also passed the written examination. My score however was five points higher than hers. We were to be interviewed by the Student Recruitment Office from the college, and they would decide which of us would be selected in terms of both the written examination and interview performance.

The girl had studied in our town school and was the first student from that school ever to meet the academic requirements of the college. If she were offered a place from the college, it would really improve the school's popularity in the district. Because of this, the town school paid great attention to her interview. Several of the school's staff members who had graduated from the college went to talk to the officials of the Student Recruitment Office. I felt the pressure from the competition. I was the first graduate of the head teacher at the boarding school who had a chance of selection, so he asked Shun whether she had any friends who could support my application. They considered my academic score to be higher than that of the girl and thought my appearance was also better. The high school was concerned that the competition should be fair. My head teacher therefore also went to talk with the officials of the Student Recruitment Office. He introduced himself as my head teacher and said that he understood they could only choose one of the two candidates. He repeated all the particulars he knew about us, including our score, height, and characteristics. He asked the officials to open the interview to an invited audience to ensure the choice was fair. The officials realized that both sides were eager to get the offer and so wanted to avoid making any mistakes.

As Shun had a friend who worked at the Education Department, she wanted to talk to her and also with the officials of the Student Recruitment Office. As there was no telephone in our town, Xia borrowed a motorbike from his colleague and drove Shun to meet them. It was a one-and-half-hour drive from our home to the city. When he was driving Shun back home, he accidentally ran over two sparrows on the way—one sparrow died and the other was unable to fly. Xia and Shun felt uncomfortable about this and worried about telling Baba, as he took these things very seriously. Baba listened quietly to what Xia said and then asked what time this had happened. Baba always used his fingers when reasoning the meaning of signs like this. Finally, he determined that as one sparrow was "executed" in the late afternoon, this was a good sign for me that I would get the offer.

The interview took place in a school with which neither of us was familiar. My teacher, Shun, and two of her friends stayed with me. I received training from Shun during the previous week on how to impress the examiners. I learned two songs and a story in preparation for what the examiners might ask. I saw the girl with her teacher and the Head Teacher of the town school. I was so nervous, but Shun told me that regardless of whatever questions they asked, just answer them in terms of my understanding. The interviews lasted 40 minutes each. Both of us were asked to sing two songs and read a 500-word text. I was also asked to do some simple physical exercises, including throwing a shot and skipping with a rope. I later found out that the examiners needed to ensure we had the potential to be a comprehensive teacher in primary school. That meant we had to be able to not only teach literature and maths but also teach music and PE.

After the interview, we had an anxious wait for the outcome. Fortunately, it was harvest time for the corn and wheat, so we were busy all day for several days. We occasionally talked about when I might hear about the offer. Mu, as she often did with important events, asked Baba to predict it. Shun was the first one to know of the outcome. I still remember it was late afternoon. I was tired as I came back from the field with Mu. As we neared home, I asked Mu "What shall we have for dinner tonight?" Then, I heard Shun's voice shouting to Mu, "Let us have nice food tonight". Shun smiled and waved an envelope in her hand, which had been left at the house. I froze, "What's this?" Shun gave me the envelope and said, "Look for yourself." I had been awarded the place! A quarter of an hour later, Baba returned home. I vividly remember the atmosphere of that late afternoon. In my hand, I held a farewell to the hoe. I would now be able to get a government salary and a city *hukou*. Baba and Mu had hoped to have another child jump out of the peasant category and now it had actually happened.

The night before I went to teacher training college, all the members of the family got together for a meal. Baba slaughtered a chicken and a duck, made tofu pudding, and also bought fish from the market. Some neighbours came to the house to congratulate me. In that year, Baba and Mu said goodbye to two of their sons—Qiu and me. He went to a distant city as a labourer, and I went to college as a student.

At college, we studied child psychology, education, lesson teaching, and how to give lectures. We also learned many practical skills a primary school teacher needed: calligraphy, playing the electric organ, drawing, dancing, and speaking Mandarin. Every month, the college gave each student a 45 RMB meal ticket to buy meals in the college cafe for the following 30 days. The meal ticket was enough in the first year, but my appetite increased from the second year onwards, so I was often hungry. I was so grateful that Xia sent me 25 RMB every month, which was a big support to cover my living expenses. Some of the girls shared their meal tickets with the boys. At traditional holidays, such as the Mid-Autumn Festival, the college provided extra meals so that all the students could get a free dish. I took an active part in different college events and became a key member of the Students Union. In my third year, I was elected President of the Students Union, and in this capacity, I participated in many social activities. Just before I graduated, I became a member of the Chinese Communist Party (CCP).

Most of us graduated when we were about 18. We were assigned to work at a primary school in a township or in the countryside; some went to schools in remote mountain villages. As we were about to graduate, news came that the cohort we had been part of at junior high school had passed the *gaokao* exam and had been admitted to university. Three years ago, the scores of these students were not as good as mine, which meant that I too could have gone on to university. Four years later, after they had graduated, these students found jobs in companies in a big city, whilst my cohort, from the teacher training college, were working as teachers in rural schools. I am sure that the girl I beat in the final interview was among those now living in the city. I was disappointed at the lost opportunity, but you have to let those things go: you can't change the past. Jumping at what seems a good opportunity at the time may mean you miss out on a better one in the future. That's life!

After graduating from college in 1996, I started working at a primary school in a town in Wenxing county.[1] When I received my first salary, I bought new clothes for Mu and Baba because I realized how much they had done to support me over the years. They were always there when I went back home at weekends to help with some of the work around the house. Baba was then living separately from Mu, but he always went to the house on Friday afternoons. On his way, he would buy some meat at the market and cook dinner to wait for my arrival. I could imagine the smell of his cooking even when I was miles away. As Kai was still living at home, the four of us would sit and enjoy the meal together.

During the day, only Mu was there, working in the fields, feeding the pigs and chickens, and preparing meals. You could be sure that whenever a family member returned and opened the door, Mu was there. I worked hard at the school, and after three years, I was promoted as assistant head teacher. I sometimes invited colleagues to come to the family home with me and have dinner. Baba would always come back to the house and, together with Mu, prepare the best food for us.

In 2000 my niece—Yu—started at the primary school in town. Yu told us all how much she liked her drawing teacher who was a recent graduate from Art College. The town primary school was fortunate to have specialist teachers in singing, dance, physical education, and drawing. At an end of term meeting for parents, Yu's mother, Lan, met this new teacher and thought that she was beautiful and patient and that she could be an excellent match for me. Lan therefore invited her and her colleagues to have a meal at her home and invited me too. I didn't know what Lan was planning, but I was happy to meet other teachers. As soon as I met Yu's teacher, I liked her and enjoyed talking with her. I found out that she was called Mei and that she was five years younger than me.

Later, I started finding different excuses to have meals with my classmates who worked at the same school as Mei. They always invited Mei to join us, and you can guess that we become good friends. Then, late afternoon one Friday, I saw Mei waiting for a bus to go back to her home in another town. I realized that the bus had already left and there was not another one due that day. I therefore offered to take her home on my motorbike. She initially hesitated because it was quite some distance, but I persisted and said that I was free and it would be my pleasure to help her. She finally accepted and climbed onto the back of my motorbike. Mei held my waist, and I concentrated on my driving. We didn't talk much during the journey because of the noise, but on the way, I made the decision that I wanted to have this lady live with me for the rest of my life. Twenty years later, I am sure that I made the right decision.

When we passed by a big store, I stopped to buy some gifts before taking her home. Mu always told us to take gifts when we first went to visit a friend. Fortunately, on that day, I had received my salary, so I had some money to spend. When we arrived at her home, it was already getting dark. Her mother thanked me for helping Mei and I gave her the fruit I had bought. Her mum invited me into the house to have a cup of tea before I returned home. I found out that Mei's mother was a businesswoman, but on that day, she was struggling with a certain problem. I overheard her talking on the telephone about the problem, and I realized that I had a friend who could help her. I offered to contact this friend and she was really pleased. Later, as a way of appreciation, Mei's mum invited me to have dinner with them one evening. As it was unsafe to ride a motorbike on the roads after dark, she invited me to stay the night. Mei was her only daughter, and she had been divorced for many years.

In the morning, I noticed that there were many small jobs that needed to be done around the house. So I asked if I could help fix some of these things. Her mum said that if it wasn't too much trouble, it would be a great help. I fixed all the things that I could see were broken, from the kitchen to the toilet. I should say that I hadn't bothered to do these jobs in my own house! The jobs took me most of the following day, and her mum stayed at home to give me any help that I needed. I think that I impressed her, and I could see she was pleased that Mei and I were friends. After we were married, she told us that on that particular weekend, she realized Mei and I liked each other and that she thought to herself that I looked like a suitable husband for her daughter. She was a smart mum, don't you think?

During the following months, every Friday, I finished work early and picked up my niece from school. Mei's friends and colleagues noticed the growing relationship between us, so whenever Mei's friends visited her, they would invite me to have a meal with them. I visited Mei's home once a month to help with some of the practical jobs around the house, and I would also cook them a big meal. Mei's mum occasionally talked with me about her business, and I would make some suggestions. I could feel that she trusted me and was supportive of our relationship, which was important for both of us. After a year, we got married, but unlike my older brothers, we didn't go through all the traditional marriage procedures. My family didn't pay any gift money, but Mei's mother did give her a big dowry. After we were married, we lived in the county town.

It was at this time that Baba died. He had been living with Chun but liked to visit Zhen every two or three days. I realized that Zhen was becoming bored of living in Jin'e, so I invited her to come and live with us in the county town. Mei has a gentle and quiet personality and she thought that Zhen was a lovely lady. However, due to Zhen's age, Mei tended to regard her more like a grandma than her mother-in-law. Mu has a strong personality, and she was very traditional in her thinking. A funny thing happened between Mu and Mei soon after Mu came to live with us. One day, Mei found that our clothes in the cupboard in our bedroom had been reorganized. Mei wondered who could have come to our bedroom! She assumed that it must have been Zhen. Mei knew I loved Mu very much, and I often encouraged her to be a good daughter-in-law like my oldest sister-in-law Lan. So Mei didn't say anything and rearranged our clothes in the way she preferred. However, in the following week, when she came home, she found that Zhen had rearranged all our clothes again. Mei suddenly realized that Zhen had arranged our clothes according to the traditional way in which the husband's clothes go in the top part of the wardrobe, and the wife's clothes are in the bottom part. Mei didn't like this way of separating clothes at different levels. Although this annoyed Mei, she didn't say anything to Zhen and quietly reorganized all the clothes. Even though they lived in the same house, neither Mei nor Zhen ever spoke about what they did. For two months, the two ladies kept changing and rearranging the clothes until finally Zhen gave up. Mei arranged our clothes according to her preferred way. When Mei told me this about a year later, I asked her why it mattered and why did she persist. She said it was useless to negotiate between modern and traditional. But Mei, with her modern ways, won.

Mei's artistic talent was soon recognized by members of the family, and they would often ask her advice on what would be the best clothes for them to buy. Now that the family had grown wealthier even Zhen started to enjoy buying new clothes. Zhen only bought clothes when Mei was staying with her because she liked to ask for Mei's suggestions about the style and colour. Some people said to Zhen, "Your grand-daughter is beautiful", then Zhen would smile and correct them, "She is my lovely daughter-in-law".

In 2006, Mei and I had a baby daughter. By now, Zhen had no preference as to whether the child would be a boy or girl, and was delighted with her new grandchild. However, during the first three days following the birth, Zhen forbade me to visit Mei with our baby in hospital. She said even though giving birth to a baby is a happy thing, blood and dirty things came out with the birth and the bad luck from these dirty things would only disappear after a week. Mu said because I am a man, the core of the family, I should avoid all this bad luck. She had argued the same thing with all her sons, much to the annoyance of their wives, but all complied out of respect for her. Mei, however, was not happy with this. I felt frustrated, as I was trying to please both Mei and Mu. I finally came up with a compromise that Mei reluctantly accepted. During the daytime, Zhen and various ladies of our family visited Mei, and in the evening after Zhen had left, I went to visit her.

Another family tradition that Zhen upheld was that if you hadn't previously stayed in her house, you shouldn't comb your hair there as it brought bad luck to the household. So, whenever any of Mei's girlfriends visited her, Zhen got annoyed if they washed their hair in our house. Shun and Lan often tried to persuade Zhen to accept the modern lifestyle rather than the old superstitions. Gradually, she did stop complaining, and Mei's friends felt freer to come and visit with their children. The house became full of noise and laughter. Perhaps it was because she was growing old that her greatest happiness was just sitting in the midst of family and children playing and chatting together.

In 2001, I was promoted to work in the county Department of Education. Quickly, life changed and became full of work and social engagements. Because both Mei and I had full-time jobs, Mei's mum offered to help to look after our little girl. She gradually reduced her business activities and moved in to live with us. After three years, I was asked to work at the local Party school as an Executive President. At that time, the Party school only provided training for the local officials. As you can guess, in a small county like ours, the number of Party officials that needed training was not large, which meant that many of the resources and facilities in the school were under-used. As the workload on the staff was only light, their salaries were not large enough for them to live on. So as to improve this situation, I actively started looking for ways of making better use of the college facilities.

From personal experience, I knew that many teachers working in primary schools and junior high schools in the county had graduated from vocational colleges and wanted to upgrade their academic qualifications. However, it was difficult for them to go to Chengdu, the provincial capital to study full time. I therefore took the initiative and contacted a university in the capital that awarded good academic qualifications. As a result of the negotiations, the university agreed to send some of their teaching staff to our county to teach at the weekends and during summer holidays. The local teachers could then finish their studies at the local Party school without interrupting their work. This programme was welcomed by many teachers and the university also benefited, as the teachers didn't take up their facilities in the city. Gradually, the collaboration of the Party school was expanded to other departments, including the local Bureau of Labour and the Personnel Bureau, which provided technical training for migrant workers.

During these years, I was free enough to play mahjong with several friends at the weekends. It was a good way to relax and build *guanxi* relationships with friends. Often, several of us families took a day out. We liked to find a farmhouse in the suburbs. Adults played mahjong together and children played games. Mei did not like playing mahjong so she was responsible for looking after the children. When I left the position at the Party school, the programmes run by the school had increased six-fold to what it was three years before. I was then asked to work as a Party Secretary in a local town not too far from Wenxing. If cadres work well in a position, the CCP is eager to see them promoted to greater responsibilities in a more important position. I was therefore pleased to be appointed to this position. The population of the town was about 54,000, and I was responsible for the town's development. After a month, I found lodgings in the town where I stayed during the week, going back home for weekends.

My colleagues and I thought about various ways that we could develop the local economy. For example, we tried to develop rural tourism and what we called "Agritainment". Agritainment was farm-based tourism in which the guests eat at a farmhouse and participate in some farming activities, such as picking fruit and vegetables, which they could take back home with them. They could also play mahjong in a rural environment and enjoy its fresh air. This style of rural tourism gave city residents a taste of rural life while helping farmers diversify their revenue. We organized farmers to visit agritainment centres near Chengdu, the provincial capital city to learn from experienced operators and improve their cooking skills and learn how to promote sales. At the same time, we raised funds to improve the road conditions in order to attract visitors to explore different villages in the area.

Several villages planted bamboo shoots and developed a bamboo mushroom industry. When customers started coming to visit the village, we made use of the village hall to display examples of the products. I asked Mei to work with the farmers and help them to display their information in a more attractive way, as she had studied exhibition design for her degree. Mei then invited her colleagues to participate in the work to support us, and this encouraged the sales of the mushrooms.

In another case, some farmers had planted pumpkins, but due to the insufficiency of sales, there were more than 40,000 pounds of pumpkins accumulating in farmers' homes during summer pumpkin harvest. After learning about the situation, I immediately contacted schools and food companies in the county in an attempt to expand their sales channels whilst negotiating a price not lower than the market rate. After a week of coordination, the pumpkins in the village were all sold out.

One Chinese New Year's Eve, it had snowed heavily and blocked the road where some villagers lived. On my way back home, I met an ambulance from the town. The medical staff stopped me and asked how they could get to one of the villages because someone there had been reported as having carbon monoxide poisoning. I immediately turned my car in that direction and took the medical staff to the village. It was nine o'clock before I got back home, and I was covered in mud from the road.

One of our biggest projects that we initiated in order to improve the living conditions of the town was to establish a natural gas system for the town. The whole project took two years and we had to overcome many difficulties, including a shortage of finance and various engineering challenges. I still remember the first day the town had access to natural gas. I was so pleased that we had finally succeeded with this project, which benefited all residents of the town. I invited all my colleagues for a big celebration. I must admit that I got very drunk and don't know how I got back home. It was only when I woke up the following morning did I realize that I was in my bed at home. It was Saturday morning, the sun was shining in the window, and I could hear Mei playing with the children and her mother cooking a meal.

* * *

Over the past 30 years, China has known rapid economic development and poverty has fallen from 73.5% in 1990 to 4.2% in 2014.[2] Nevertheless, in 2013, there were still more than 70 million people in rural communities living below the poverty line. The government has vowed to lift these people out of poverty by 2020, so unlike previous measures, its policy specifically targets poor villages, households, and individuals. In the town where I work, we have not only surveyed all the households and villages but also set specific targets to improve the general infrastructure. We want each village to have some form of stable industry and each house to have vehicular access. These requirements have proved really challenging. The good news however is that each village is now in contact with the Enterprise Department of the local town to which they can go directly to receive help; and our town is in contact with the Enterprise Department at the provincial level. As a leader of the town, I have been involved in all these projects, and I am pleased that we are beginning to see positive results.

The countryside is changing! Jin'e is different from what I remember as a child. I can't imagine how different it is from when Mu was a little girl. Mu continues to live alternatively with Chun and me. She stays with me for three or four weeks and then goes to live with Chun for another three or four weeks. Both our families have a room that we keep especially for her. She asks Jiang, her oldest grandson, to drive her the 40-minute journey between our two houses. Once a year, Mu also likes to visit Qiu in Guangzhou and sometimes stays with him for a couple of months. We think that she is funny because she is always careful to select a lucky date for her journey to Guangzhou, as she believes this will bring her good luck during her stay. Mu is worried that if she dies in Guangzhou, her body will be cremated and so will not be returned to be buried alongside Baba in Jin'e. To me, Mu represents the remnants of old China with her superstitions and customs, old ways that will soon be gone forever. I am pleased that the poverty and ignorance have gone but sad that Mu's generation, which suffered so much, will soon be no more.

Notes

1. The local government in China consists of five levels: provincial (province, autonomous region, municipality, and special administrative region), prefecture (*Shi*, 市), county (*Xian*, 县), township (*Xiangzhen*, 乡镇), and village (*Cun*, 村).
2. China Daily (2015). "Poverty alleviation to help unleash potential of domestic consumption". *China Daily*. Beijing.

CHAPTER 11

Grandma Remembers

"Grandma come this way!" My children and grandchildren fuss over me as they lead me into the room they had reserved in one of the best restaurants in town. "Sit here," calls Chun, my eldest boy, as he offers me the chair at the place of honour at the big round table. My sons and daughters, with their wives and husbands, take their seats amidst much chatter and laughter.

This is one of our family meals we have on special occasions. Today is 24th December of the lunar year 2017. This day is called *Xiaonian*, which means a small celebration for the Spring Festival. It is also my birthday. I am wearing an expensive red wine-coloured coat Xia bought for me, and Mei, my youngest daughter-in-law, has combed my white hair to make it nice and tidy. Before dinner starts, Chun stands up and gives a toast to me. "Today is Mum's 85th birthday and I represent all my sisters and brothers in wanting to show our appreciation for all the love she has given to us. During hard times Mum's endurance and perseverance has encouraged us to overcome the difficulties we faced. Let us celebrate Mum's birthday together and look forward to a good year to come."

The waiters then start bringing in plates of delicious food: steamed turtle, fried shrimp, chicken soup, green vegetables, and lots of others. The family laugh and chat amidst the toasts they offer each other. My children toast me, and my youngest daughter Kai says, "While Mu is alive, we, brothers and sisters, come together as a family, but once she dies we will only be relatives as we will no longer have a Baba or a Mu to unite us."

Kai is probably right—when I am gone, what will bring all my children back together like this? My 11 grandchildren come as a group to toast me. Some of them now have jobs while others are still studying at university or high school. I am happy they all have a much better life than Baba and I did, and their prospects are even better than their own parents at their age.

My youngest brother, nieces, and nephews have also been invited to join the gathering. I haven't seen my brother for two years; his back is more bent now but otherwise he looks healthy. As I told you at the beginning of my story, I had two brothers but the oldest one who did so much to support our family died 20 years ago.

Outside it is cold, but the room is hot and noisy, full of chatter and laughter, which is how we like to celebrate special days. I can't help smiling to myself at how things have changed for us as a family. In the years of hunger, my dream was that all my children would live. Now they are not only alive, but they have plenty of food, nice clothes, and a decent place to live. Some of the family are even keeping to a diet in order to lose weight. I never thought they would ever have the life they live today. The children kindly spoon morsels of food into my bowl and encourage me to eat. How the world has changed!

I remember the hungry times when even a scrap of food was precious, but here we all sit with many plates of food. As there is too much for us to eat, we will take the surplus food home with us in "doggy bags" to eat tomorrow. Previously surplus food was thrown away, but recently the media has publicized that people should "empty their plate" to stop wasting food. Hmm, I think that this is very good, but it should have been introduced earlier. I notice that there is a dish of sweet potato. In the hard times, sweet potatoes maintained our lives; without it, we wouldn't have survived. Chun still doesn't like sweet potato—he says that he ate more than enough as a child.

Chun is sitting next to me, with his wife, Lan, next to him. Chun is a good man and has done well as the head of the family through some difficult times. He is a cadre in the town government responsible for animal husbandry and veterinary work. He has integrity and is trusted by people in the community. You can see that because he is always invited to coordinate town affairs. Lan has been a good wife to him. She now stays at home to look after me and cook for Chun. She grows some vegetables, as she says it is good exercise for her and we can always enjoy fresh vegetables from our land. When she is gardening, I like to sit on the land, watching her and enjoying the sunshine. If neighbours are in need, she is always kind and quick to give them support. Chun and Lan's daughter is now working at a university, but she returns to visit us during the summer holidays and Spring Festival. I don't understand all the subjects that my grandchildren study, but I always knew that education would be important if our family was going to progress.

Next to them sits Shun with her husband, Ze. Although I had wanted a boy for my first born, Shun has proved to be a very special daughter and led the family well until Chun was married and could take over as head of the family. The opportunity she had to study at the teacher training college proved to be so important for us as a family. Shun was always good at her studies and liked to read even if the light was poor; that was probably what damaged her eyesight. It also helped that our little house was opposite the commune offices and that I taught Shun always to be helpful to the officials, and she was. I am sure that this was one of the reasons she was chosen to study at the college. The officials knew that our family was poor and could see we were kind and hard working. In Chairman Mao's time, this was important because he said that all Chinese should learn from the peasants. That was us! Even though I didn't know what educated city people could learn from poor people like us, the policy made it possible for Shun to become an official teacher with a decent salary. She was the first person in our family to be more than a peasant. This chance not only changed her identity but opened a new door for the family. Cheng and I firmly believed that no matter how difficult things are, to be hard working and kind-hearted is the basis of a good life.

Shun and Ze were a good match, and they were able to support each other and help with the education of my younger children. When Ze first came to our family, he was a teenager, unrelated to us. Now he is 65 and has been my son-in-law for 40 years. Ze and Shun are happy looking after their second grandchild. After the one-child policy stopped in 2015, they welcomed a second grandchild. Shun and Ze are not rich, but both of them have adequate pensions. They still like to visit the village where they worked and sometimes stay there for a few days. Their son works in the town government, and their daughter studied overseas and has a doctoral degree. When I asked what a "doctoral degree" means, they said it is the topmost level and end of the education process. I don't believe that there is an end to learning, but I don't voice my opinions. You know, they are all educated while I still don't know my letters. I remember that Shun gave birth to her daughter—her second child—when the one-child policy was still in place, and how I cared for her when she was a tiny baby and brought her up.

Anyway, everyone seems to think highly of her and what she has achieved, and I am proud of her because she is my granddaughter.

I am also pleased that Hua, my third daughter, and her husband are reconciled and back in the family. She now cultivates the family fields and her husband works as a security man for a private company. The four-storied house they built now looks somewhat old and shabby. The baby Hua had when she thought she was past the age has grown into a lovely girl. She has a good academic record and a full scholarship to study in high school. They expect so much of her. I hope that they don't put too much pressure on her as perhaps I did with my children. When the girl was in primary school, they often suggested how she should do her studies, but when she went to high school, she sometimes rejected them because she thought their ideas were out-of-date. I tell Hua, don't interfere too much with your daughter's studies; patience and encouragement is the best approach a parent can use to help their child's education. I think Hua and her husband now realize they should not intervene. Perhaps it is because she has done so well that they feel she knows now more than them. I am so pleased girls have the same chance to go to school as boys.

Xia, my second son and his wife, are busy with their business. They tell me that the authorities are building a high-speed railway from Chengdu to Guiyang, capital of Guizhou Province. This will pass near Jin'e and it will open in 2019. It will then only take one-and-a-half hours to get from here to Chengdu. I remember the 12-hour bus journey that Cheng and I took when we first went to Chengdu to visit Qiu some 20 years ago. I cannot believe it will be so quick to travel all that way! Xia is excited about this, as he thinks that the railway will bring them a lot of new business. Recently, neighbours have come to congratulate me because their son has been offered a place at one of the best universities in the world. I have no idea what makes one university better than another, but I am pleased for him. As a child, I just wanted to go to school with my brothers, but now the family wants the best universities for their children.

Kai, my youngest daughter, is the leader of the Ladies Association. She likes social activities and is concerned about women's rights. If she knows any woman has been beaten by her husband, she gets angry and always helps her. It's funny she sometimes says she is my leader because I am an automatic member of the Ladies Association. She says if any of my sons are not nice enough to me, she can help safeguard my legal rights. Ha-ha! If she were to criticize her brothers to safeguard my rights, it would bring shame on the family. She spends much of her time on her work but worries about her daughter's academic performance; she hopes her daughter will soon have an offer from a good university. I am so happy Kai has a good relationship with her husband.

Qiu is here! Every year, he returns to the county town for the Spring Festival but never goes to Jin'e. He also doesn't like to stay with any members of the family, preferring to stay in a hotel. I can understand the reason for this after all that happened to him in the past. I know he still remembers the time I shouted at him for coming at the bottom of his class and told him to get out of the house. It was the only way I could think of to make him get on with his studies. He is sad at the way he was misunderstood and punished by his teachers, and how he had to run away from the village. The scars of those teenage years remain in his memory. I sometimes wonder if I didn't treat him in the best way, but in those hard times, I didn't think I had any other choice. Oh well, that's life! Fortunately, he has learnt the importance of working hard and he does work hard.

He left Jin'e in 1990. Baba and I were so sad to see him walk away that night, and we didn't realize that it would be many years before we would see him again. I know that at first life in the city was difficult for him. I was pleased when he met Ju and married and had twin boys. Ju is a nice young woman. Even after they divorced, I still regard her as part of our family. I hope that one day, she will find a kind man and marry again. After Qiu divorced, he re-married and now has another boy.

The boy Qiu fought with those years ago now lives in the next county where he works as a policeman. We don't see anything of him. I heard that his sister went to a city far away and died at a young age. As I always say, "The bodhisattva has eyes."[1] Maybe they have been punished for the bad things they did in the past.

My second daughter Shi is not here. Although she was not good at school, she was a hard worker, and when she was young, she was a great help to me looking after her younger brothers and sisters. She was a good tailor and was kind to Chun and Xia when they were at school. I always smile when I remember the time she saved her youngest brother from the cesspit and how proud the boys were when she made them new shirts. However, I can understand why her brothers and sisters don't want to speak to her anymore because of the way she duped Baba. As a proverb says, "both the palm and the back of the hand are fleshy." Nevertheless for me, they are all my children and I can't choose which one to keep and which one to abandon. It is sad they are divided like this, but what can I do? When no one is around, I pop round to her house, which is next to

Chun's for a chat. Shi always quietly passes a little gift to me: She is my girl. If Chun and Lan actually know I go to see her, they don't say anything and neither do I.

I know all my children think I was hard on them when they were young for not allowing them to play with other children. We were not a city family with their privileges, and I knew that it would only be through hard work we would ever progress. To work hard was what Chairman Mao encouraged us all to do. Although I wanted all my children, both boys and girls, to go to school, I also thought that each of them should learn some practical skills. I encouraged them to be kind to other people, especially to those who supported us in our most difficult times. You can see how well they have done. I didn't mind all the hard work I did for them and sacrificing my life so that they could have a better life. For a poor peasant woman, this is the only gift you can give to your children.

I often tell my children, we not only give birth to the next generation but we raise them too. Sometimes, I hear them saying to their own children what I used to say to them: "Don't let your hands be idle." Whenever my grandchildren come to visit me, I always wish they could stay longer, as I don't know when I shall see them again, but they have to leave and continue with their lives. They have their study and work to do so they can have a good life. My greatest hope is that my grandchildren will study and work hard. They don't necessarily have to be excellent students, but they should make the best effort they can.

In recent years, my grandchildren have made foreign friends and some have come to stay with us for a few days. They called me *Popo*, which means Grandma. The first time a foreign visitor called me "*Popo*", it felt so strange. I remember the time I tried to speak to the foreigner—I spoke very slowly because I know people from the cities have a different accent to me. My granddaughter asked me, "Do you think she can understand what you said?" I know it is difficult for a foreigner, and that is why I am speaking so slowly to her. My granddaughter asked me, "Can you understand what she said?" All I could understand was *Popo*. My granddaughter said her foreign friend had also spoken slowly in Chinese. I don't understand: *Mi* is *Mi* and *Rou* is *Rou*.[2] Why do these foreign people call them differently? Never mind, I can always use gestures and smiles. When you don't know what to say, just smile; that is always a good choice.

I am sorry that Cheng is not here to see how well our children have done. On Tomb Sweeping Day, Shun or Chun take me to visit Cheng's grave on the mountainside, and I tell him everything that has happened in the family during the past year. Chun has already prepared a grave for me just next to Cheng. It is in a lovely spot, looking down the valley over the fields and water. I told Cheng that I had travelled to Hong Kong, Macao, and even to Tiananmen Square in Beijing where I saw the crystal sarcophagus of Chairman Mao. I told Cheng that Chun has a new house, which has three toilets. That's really a waste, don't you think? I am sorry that Cheng wasn't able to enjoy the good life we have today. Sometimes, I dream of him and he tells me about his life in the after-world. He says he worked so hard to support us all in life, and now he is lonely on his own. Whenever it is the auspicious time, I burn some paper money for him. I miss him so much.

Cheng died in 1997 when he was 72. He was eight years older than me and had to suffer a great deal in his life. In his later years, he had TB, which the doctors said was due to him smoking too much. That was true. Every morning, you would see him puffing on his pipe. Cheng was in hospital for two months, and when he came out, he was never in good health again. Towards the end, we lived separately for two years; he was often cross and we'd argue, so I told him I didn't want him to visit me. He must have been so sad about what I said. Then one day, he returned to Chun's house and never came back. He had a stroke in the toilet at Chun's house and died quickly. In life, we never know when a goodbye will become the last goodbye and when you will never see your loved one alive again. After he died, I was so sad, but I had to be strong because Kai, Qiu, and Dong were still single, and I needed to provide them with a home to which they could return.

There are still a few people of my generation living in Jin'e. Over the years, many died during the famine, or in childbirth, or simply through the stress of overwork, illness, and ageing. About half the old women live on their own, as all their children have gone to work in the cities and they only see them in the spring holidays. Occasionally, we meet in the market and chat, but actually we are all lonely. I am fortunate to be living with Chun and Lan, and my children always give me money and buy clothes for me at special festivals. But, they are all busy and when they do come to visit, they don't have long to stay and talk with me. I miss them!

Last year, I had trouble with the veins in my legs and Qiu suggested I had surgery in Guangzhou. I was in a deep coma for several hours for the operation, and then I heard Qiu calling to me "Mu, Mu", and I woke up. When I opened my eyes, Qiu's head was next to mine and he looked so worried. I looked around the hospital room and I saw that there were only

Qiu and a doctor. I suddenly felt sad and lonely. I thought if I hadn't woken up from the operation, only Qiu would have been there to say goodbye to me even though I had brought up eight children. Qiu begged me to live with him in Guangzhou and said that he would employ a carer to look after me, but I refused. I know that he is busy with his work, and so when I stay with him, I am usually on my own during the day and only see him in the late evening. I don't like staying in the city where I don't know anybody. I like living with Chun and Lan because I know many people in the town, and I can talk with people on the street and listen to Lan's nagging.

Another thing that makes me sad is that the younger generation doesn't want to follow the old traditions. Sometimes, I get taken to the little temple up on the hill. It was partly destroyed by the Red Guard but was rebuilt some years ago. It is a nice, quiet place away from the noise of traffic. Even so, not many people go there; some people regard it as superstition. I like to go and kneel and offer incense to the gods and pray for my family. Some of the other older people like to sit there and chat. The temple was an important part of the life I knew as a child—perhaps that is why I like to go there and see the familiar statues.

Every family now has a TV and computers, but I don't really like them. When the Spring Festival comes, my grandchildren sit watching TV or play computer games separately, rather than talking or playing games with each other. I still remember when the family bought our first TV and we all sat together around this small black and white TV set. We really enjoyed that time! Today, my grandchildren sometimes watch the English language channel; I enjoy sitting with them even though I don't understand any of the words. I just like being with them. Chun has now given me a cell phone and set the phone numbers so that even though I can't read I know which button to press for each of my children. For me, things have moved so quickly, and I am too old now to learn to read or drive a car. I am glad that many things have changed, but I have struggled to become part of this new way of life. Anyway, I am happy my children and grandchildren can enjoy their life.

These days my memory is not as good as it used to be. I think of things I want to do, but then I forget what they were. Lan is always there to help me remember what I was about to do. My vision also has got worse and I feel my eyes are covered with a veil. The world has become unclear for me. I know I am getting older.

Past days are now beginning to fade, but the scenes of the struggles and joys still remain as clear as ever. Although I never learned to read or write, I did learn how to do business from my father. Oh, that was long, long ago! By going to the market with him, I learned how to run a little business, amongst other things. I realized that I had to get up early to find a good place in the market. I saw how my father dealt with his customers to get a good bargain, how to make a profit, and how to leave the customer happy with what they had bought. This experience taught me a lot, and I wanted to teach my children how to be successful in business too. I will never forget the days of hunger and the way that Shun and Shi, as little girls, shivered in the cold in their thin clothes. I wish that I could have done more for them. I sometimes remember the fourth child I gave birth to, who died when she was only a few days old. She was such a tiny thing, but I didn't have the milk to feed her. Even in the most difficult days, I was convinced that one should hold onto life with all one's strength because this is the only way to have a future; where there is food there is life, where there is life there is hope.

Now, I don't have to worry about food and clothes anymore. I don't need to be anxious about whether the harvest will be good this year, if there is enough food in the store, or how I can pay the tuition fees for the children. Nevertheless, when spring comes, I like to go to the fields to look at the seedlings growing. These growing seedlings have each year given us life.

I like to visit Shun and see my great-granddaughter playing the piano. She is nine years old and clever too. Yesterday afternoon, I fell asleep on the sofa while she was playing the piano. I dreamed I was nine and was following my father as he went to do business in town. On the road, we met Cheng, who was then an apprentice, following his master. He greeted us with a big smile, and I lowered my eyes as I felt shy. When I awoke, the house was silent. My great-granddaughter was sitting next to me, quietly reading a book.

My lifetime has witnessed the rapid development of China. It has moved from war to peace, from poverty to riches, from being closed to being open. There have been many tears and joys. I know, one day, I will have to say goodbye to my children and grandchildren. I like hearing the laughter as they sit around the table eating and drinking. I know I will not have this for many more years, but still, I am content!

Notes

1. A bodhisattva in Chinese traditional religion is an enlightened being who looks down and helps those in need.
2. In Chinese, *mi* is rice 米, and *rou* is meat 肉.

CHAPTER 12

Anthropological Themes

Grandma Zhen and her generation have experienced unbelievable changes in their lifetime. As a young wife and mother, she only wanted her family to survive and hopefully prosper. Life has changed in ways she could never have imagined. She now sees the optimism and ambition of the younger generation and hopes that they will indeed fulfil their dreams. Like many of her generation, she is grateful to be guided by her children and grandchildren through the maze of modern life. She doesn't know what their lives will become in the great cities of the world. But she wants her story to be told so that her grandchildren and great-grandchildren may know that their roots are in the soil of a little village in a distant part of China.

In this final chapter, we explore five aspects of the life of Chinese peasants that can be seen in this study and the struggles many have had in adjusting to change. Whilst the circumstances of Zhen's family are typical, we do not claim that her family is representative of rural Chinese families as a whole. However, the stories do illustrate how rural families have experienced and adapted to the immense social changes that have occurred during their lifetimes.

THE FAMILY

It was the famous Chinese anthropologist Fei Xiaotong who in 1936 made what was the first academic study of life in a Chinese village (Fei Xiaotong 1939). In discussing the family, he wrote "The basic social group of the village is the *Jia*, an extended family.... The term family, as commonly used by anthropologists, refers to the procreative unit consisting of parents and immature children. A *Jia* is essentially a family but it sometimes includes children even when they have grown and married. Sometimes it also includes some relatively remote patrilineal kinsmen" (Fei Xiaotong 1983). As the various stories show, this was the traditional pattern of Chinese family life until 1949 when the Chinese Communist Party (CCP) came to power and radical changes began to pull the family apart.

As Jankowia and Moore have reminded us, the traditional Chinese family followed the Confucian ethic of filial piety in which older family members had authority over younger members (Jankowia and Moore 2016). Filial piety encourages the younger generation to follow the teaching of elders and elders to teach the young their duties and manners. The patrilineal nature of the Confucian ethic meant that the head of any *Jia* was the oldest male whose most important relationship was with his son and not his wife. As Yan writes, "The centrality of the father-son relationship derived from the belief in patrilineal descent, whereby living individuals are nothing more than the personification of all their forebears and all their descendants (including those yet to be born)" (Yan 2011: 213).

Although wealthy families were often quite large, with as many as 30 people of three or four generations living together, most peasant families consisted of only five or six people. Each household worked essentially as a little commercial enterprise characterized by a common budget, shared property, and a household economy with a strict pooling of income. It could advance or decline economically and socially depending on how successful they were in coping with bad weather, ill health, and a multitude of social events. As a result, peasant families should not be considered as a uniformly impoverished mass. Cheng and Zhen's early family history illustrates some of the struggles that a peasant family faced, which sometimes required extreme actions merely for them to survive. The long-term goal of the head of the family was to ensure the survival and prosperity of the family and to pass the assets on to the following generation. In Zhen's family, she and Cheng hoped to have a son early in their marriage to acquire Cheng's skill as a vet. When Chun, their first son was 12 years old, he worked as an apprentice to Cheng.

The headship of the family was normally taken over by the eldest son soon after his marriage. He continued to live in the family house where his bride would come to live with him. In Zhen's case, her oldest child was a girl, Shun, and her first son was not born until eight years later, so Shun took on the role of head of the *Jia* until her brother Chun was old enough to marry. This was unusual at the time, but Shun was different for at least two other reasons.

First, she was the most educated member of the family with a salaried government job. Second, her husband was the only child (by adoption) of his parents so they did not have to spend much time dealing with matters relating to his parents. Thus Zhen and Cheng considered it appropriate for her to take the leadership of the family until their first son married. When eventually Chun married his wife, Lan left her own *jia*, came to live at Chun's family house, and became a member of his *jia*.

Because the eldest son took over as the head of the family, marriage was a family matter, and even in the twentieth century, parents had a fairly free hand in arranging the marriages of their sons and daughters. Nonetheless, parents were concerned to find a partner for their son or daughter who would be approved of by their child as well as themselves. Who wants to have a young couple living in the house if they continually argue? Zhen was therefore eager to ensure that her future daughter-in-law would make a good, hard-working partner for her eldest son.

In 1950, the People's Republic of China (PRC) introduced the Marriage Law, which aimed at replacing the "feudal" patriarchal marriage system with the "new democratic" marriage system. The new law prohibited bigamy, child betrothal, and demands for money and gifts in connection with marriage. A couple no longer depended on parents to arrange their marriage but could, by mutual consent, register their wish to marry with the local government office. The individual was therefore released from the traditional constraints of the family, but these became replaced by the new restraints of the commune and ultimately by the socialist state.

In general, the family reforms were more accepted in urban regions, while in the countryside, there was a combination of continuity and change. As these stories show, Zhen's family wanted their children's marriages to retain some of the traditional social customs, including the role of the matchmaker and the fortune-teller. Zhen was quite adamant that the parents of a young man expressing an interest in one of her daughters would ask a matchmaker to approach them. Likewise, she would ask a matchmaker to approach the parents of a young woman to propose she became the wife of her son. The chief considerations in the selection of a suitable bride were usually threefold: physical health (to ensure children), hard working (to contribute to the family income), and a pleasant manner (to ensure household harmony). If both families were willing, the marriage process would move on to the next stage. This stage involved the fortune-teller, who was given the eight characters defining the year, month, date, and hour of birth of both parties to assess their compatibility.

Traditionally, gifts were exchanged between the families to build mutual relationships. The man's family gave the gift of a bride-price to the girl's family. From an economic point of view, marriage is a disadvantage to the girl's parents because as soon as she is mature and can assume her full share of work, she is taken to the man's family. For this reason, parents of girls did not want to spend their resources on their daughter's schooling as was seen in Zhen's story. However, Zhen ensured that all her daughters had an equal chance as her sons to go to school, which was encouraged by the change in the national policy (Cleverley 1991). The girl's family would also provide a dowry to help establish the young couple, which often consisted of personal belongings, bedding, furniture, and so on. The new couple would then have a room, furnished more or less, for themselves in the parental home. From the bride's point of view, whenever she returns to her parent's home, she is now only a guest in that house. Within the various marriage rituals, showing respect to the ancestors of the new *jia* was important for the young bride (Ebrey 1991). The expense of a traditional wedding was excessive for many poor farmers, and for this reason, after the first wedding, Shun took the view that, because there were so many younger siblings, henceforth marriages should be kept simple with minimal expense.

A related issue is *fenjia*—"division of the family". The process of division was one of the most important steps in the transmission of property from parents to children, especially for larger families. Through the process, the young gain legal title over part of the property and responsibility for the care of parents and younger siblings. With four sons, this process was especially important for Zhen's family, as was seen in Chap. 7. The division occurs amongst the married sons, with the eldest son usually getting the largest share, but interestingly, this was not so in Chun's case, as the property was divided into four fairly equal parts. Unmarried sons continue to live with the parents and can demand a share when they are married. The actual process of division can take different forms depending upon whether the parents are still living, the size of the house, or whether the family had prepared for the division by building another house. The concept of *fenjia* has therefore gradually disappeared, like the concept of the head of the *jia*, but respect for elderly parents is still important.

As we will show, with the Reform and Opening-Up under Deng Xiaoping in 1979, the restraints of the commune were removed and individuals suddenly found social conditions that enabled them to have new opportunities outside the socialist system. As Yan (2010) points out, the rise in the importance of the individual and the consequential individualization in China is part of the State's sponsored quest for modernity. Those couples who still lived with the husband's parents nonetheless found their own ways to cultivate intimate and strong conjugal bonds that favoured youth autonomy over parental authority. This is seen in Lan's struggle to adjust to married life with Chun, and also Fang's struggles. By the early 1990s, a strong husband-wife relationship had become an accepted feature of family life, and horizontal conjugal ties had replaced vertical parent-son relationships as the central axis of family relations in most rural families. In Zhen's family, the adult children of the third generation now rarely return to the family home to live with their parents, but visit them during the holidays. It is now more likely that the parents go to live with their children and look after the grandchildren whilst both parents are working full time.

The descriptions of marriage discussed in these stories occurred among the second generation, between 1970 and 1995. During this century, new patterns of love and courtship have emerged in China (Yunxiang Yan 2002). Young people are now able to use mobile phones or social media to keep in touch, whether they remain in the village or are scattered in different areas of the country. In Zhen's family, the third generation, her grandchildren are approaching marriageable age. They prefer to choose their own partners and marry when they are older, about 30. The traditional marriage customs have disappeared, and it is rare that a matchmaker or a fortune-teller is involved. However, in most towns and cities, there is a park or a community space in which parents or grandparents congregate with photographs of their young people, hoping to find parents and grandparents who are also looking to find a suitable match for their child.

Whilst at school, parents focus their child's attention on the dreaded *gaokao* examination, but once at university, relationships can bloom. At university, students live in dorms with five or six other students, but sexual relations can occur using hotel rooms conveniently located near the colleges. Young migrant workers, like Qiu, usually live in dorms and are required to work long hours. Nevertheless, this does not stop them from developing relationships in their free time. Young people often choose to live together for a period of time before they get married. It is also relatively easy for two people to break up because of their personalities whilst living together. They usually consider marriage when they are in full-time employment and own an apartment by means of a mortgage. Parents have also become more understanding of these practices. People living in the cities tend to live in close proximity to both sets of parents, what Fong and Kim have called "networked families" (Fong and Kim 2011: 1102).

Land Reform and Social Mobility

In the 1940s, about 80% of the population of China were peasant farmers and land was fundamental to their life. Most peasant families owned no land, but rented land from a landowner and were free to decide what to plant and how to use the labour of the family members. The wife was expected to be concerned with children and household activities whilst the husband was more involved with external activities. It can be seen that Zhen's father went out to work whilst her mother stayed home to look after the children and the home. Because of her bound feet, she was unable to work in the fields. When Zhen married, she focused upon farming and household activities and Cheng worked as a vet.

With the establishment of the PRC in 1949, one of the most significant policy changes was related to land ownership. In traditional land tenure, land was considered to be divided into two layers: the surface and the subsoil. The possessor of the subsoil was registered with the government as the title holder of the land. The owner could either cultivate the land or lease it out to others. The owner of the surface without the subsoil is the tenant, and this was always held by the *jia* (Fei Xiaotong 1939: 177). Even two years before the foundation of the PRC, the CCP launched land reform campaigns in the villages it controlled in northern China. This was extended nationwide in 1949. The programme transferred vast areas of land from landlords and rich farmers to poor peasants, resulting in a large number of family farms. Zhen, like other poor peasants, was excited to be allocated land in 1951, which she understood as her "share of the victory" (Ruf 1998: 93). However, the land was soon brought under a new collective with the "agricultural cooperation movement". The government encouraged peasants to cooperate together by sharing farm tools and animals. This later developed into the commune system, with communal kitchens and work teams, and eventually resulted in the famine of 1959–60.

A new pattern of authority emerged with the formation of the Party through many levels from national leadership to the local village Party Secretary. The number of Party members increased as members of the Peoples' Liberation Army and peasants applied and took active roles. The system resulted in a lifetime tenure system that has become fundamental to China's bureaucracy since 1949. The cadre (*ganbu*) system roughly functions as does the civil service system in Western countries. The term cadre refers to a public official holding a responsible or managerial position, usually full time, in the Party and government. The state not only pays salaries but also provides social benefits, which range from gifts at public festivals and holidays to welfare and retirement plans. This became known as the "iron rice bowl" and for peasants provided a means of escape from agricultural work. Shun's story (Chap. 2) tells how she was the first of the family to move into such a role and was followed by Chun (Chap. 6) and later Yan (Chap. 10).

The restructuring of the rural economy caused a considerable diversification of peasant households. The traditional pattern of men working the land ("outside") while women took care of domestic duties ("inside") changed. Few households remained completely reliant on agriculture and most diversified into various domestic side-lines, such as starting small businesses or seeking work in large towns or cities. Agricultural work in the fields was taken over for most of the year by women, children, and the elderly, while many men became migrant workers. Wives who established their own businesses were seen as making a major contribution to family finances and gained both respect and authority within the family. However, such women often continued to carry their traditional responsibilities for housework, childcare, and care for the elderly. This is seen in many of the stories recounted in the previous chapters.

Even as early as the mid-1950s, labour migration to the cities was seen as an urgent national problem, and new regulations were passed to stop the uncontrolled flow. This was enforced by the Household Registration Stipulations of 1958, which required every Chinese citizen to be registered at birth with the local authorities as either having an urban or a rural *hukou* (household registration). Rural *hukou* holders are prohibited from migrating to the cities and are not entitled to receive state-subsidized housing, food, education, medical care, and employment, which are reserved for urban *hukou* holders. This stopped the growth of vast slums common in many developing countries. Although during the Cultural Revolution, millions of Red Guards, mostly urban youth, travelled to various cities and especially to Beijing; this was not seen in terms of population migration but as a political event.

A third land reform that introduced the family-based contract system known as the "Household Responsibility System" began in 1979. Although land use rights were returned to individual farmers, collective land ownership was left undefined after the people's communes were disbanded. Since 1983, the government has introduced a series of land policy reforms to improve land use efficiency, to rationalize land allocation, to enhance land management, and to coordinate urban and rural development. The most telling impact of these changes was the release of the rural workers from the land, which was often called *songbang*, "to untie". "The rural reform programmes including the most radical decollectivization were nothing more than the untying of the peasant from the constraints of the collectives and allowing them to work as individual labourers" (Kleinman 2011: 14).

There were an estimated two million labour migrants in 1980, and by 2006, the number had grown to 132 million. As more and more poured into the cities, they came to be seen as a social problem. Two important documents were issued: "State Council Notification on the Question of Peasants Entering Towns" (1984) and "Provisional Regulations on the Management of the Population Living Temporarily in the Cities" (1985). Official attempts to regulate migration did not stop millions of peasants from entering the cities because the growing urban economy needed migrant labour for building projects and low-skilled jobs. Beginning in the early 1990s, migrants nationwide had to apply for a temporary residence card from the local police station if they intended to stay in the city for more than a month. In May 1995, the "Application Procedures for Temporary Residence Cards" was enacted, which required that all migrants register with the local authorities. Anyone 16 or older who intended to stay somewhere other than his or her own *hukou* residence for more than a month had to obtain a renewable temporary residence card (*zhanzhu zheng*) valid for a maximum of one year. Since that time, many books have been written on the so-called floating population of migrants, including Li Zhang's more academic text *Strangers in the City* (Li Zhang 2001) and Leslie Chang's story of the lives of two young women *Factory Girls* (Chang 2010). Tamara Jacka in her book *Rural Women in Urban China* (Jacka 2006) shows that women migrate for various reasons—to experience new things, to escape rural life, or to follow their dreams. Like Qiu's first wife (Chap. 9), few wanted to return to the countryside. The few who did return wanted to use their newly acquired skills learnt in the city to set up a business to improve the condition of their families.

In a speech in August 1980 entitled "On the Reform of the Party and State Leadership System", Deng Xiaoping declared that power was over-centralized and concentrated in the hands of individuals who followed patriarchal methods in carrying out their duties. Deng criticized the bureaucracy as operating without the benefit of regularized and institutionalized procedures, and he recommended corrective measures. In 1981, Deng proposed that a younger, better-educated leadership be recruited from among cadres in their 40s and 50s who had trained at colleges or technical secondary schools. This reorientation required the massive retirement of many veteran cadres and the recruitment of younger cadres knowledgeable in economics and technology to be trained in leadership positions. It was an enormous task and one that obviously met significant resistance from those who either did not understand the new requirements or saw them as a substantial threat to their own position and livelihood.

In the countryside, the Party searches for the best scholars for training at vocational colleges so that they would take on significant roles in local leadership. Shun was one of the earliest chosen for training as a primary school teacher. Later, Chun had a chance to train as a veterinarian to help improve farming in the local community. The events in the lives of Qiu and Dong (third and fourth sons) also illustrate how young people were affected by their academic results. As we have seen, whilst Dong had the opportunity to study and a government paid position, Qiu had to leave for the city to find his own way.

The opportunity to set up a private business was another result of the "Reform and Opening-Up", which by 1982 was affecting all the villages. In the early 1980s, Ze (Chap. 3) had to find a new job when the commune store closed. At the time, government policy lacked clarity as to how and where people could start their own businesses. As there was no shop in the village, Ze decided to open his own shop but remained prepared for the possibility that the authorities might ask for it to be closed. Fortunately, the policy was soon clarified and Ze's shop continued doing good business.

The new policy gave exciting opportunities for enterprising people like Ze. In order to succeed, these new entrepreneurs needed to have a reasonable level of education, skills in buying and selling commodities, and above all a willingness to take advantage of the new opportunities and the risks involved. Throughout the country, people took up these opportunities—some succeeded and some failed. Many who failed in one business took up a second one or a third. It was those who were willing to work incredibly hard, take risks, and always be on the lookout for new possibilities who succeeded. Shi (second daughter) was an example of this. She was on the lookout for new opportunities and set up a shop in the village soon after her husband was appointed village head. By 1994, she was pleased to be the wealthiest of Zhen's children. Zhen's second son, Xia, also started his own business selling agricultural products.

Nevertheless, new opportunities carried challenges. Hua's husband, Guang, had studied some medicine when he was in the army, and although he was not a qualified doctor, he had been taught how to make up prescriptions (Chap. 5). In 1989, Hua and Guang set up a small pharmacy in town, where they not only sold medicines but also toilet paper and similar commodities. The business started off well, as they offered a needed service to the village. Then, at the beginning of this century, the government introduced changes to its health care policy; each village was to have a qualified doctor under whose direction all medicines had to be sold. So Hua and Guang's business was effectively over. By 2014, each village has a medical centre responsible for basic medical services under the administration of the Department of Health.

Success in business and the increase in consumer products brought about the growth of a middle class, which didn't exist during the Maoist period. Business people started from a rather low status in the early 1980s when the private sector was considered a useful complement to the planned economy. Gradually, business people have emerged as a new and powerful social group that is much admired. This has grown to about 200 million in 2008 and is estimated to reach 520 million by 2025 (Li 2010).

As we have seen, Chinese society emphasizes relationships far more than Western society. This relational capital is known as *guanxi* and implies trust, understanding, and accountability. The opportunity to study for Shun, the work opportunities of Kai and Xia, and the business opportunity of Chun, all came from relationships. *Guanxi* places the moral obligations that stem from personal relationships above other considerations. Nevertheless, *guanxi* has its limits; like other tenets of Chinese culture, the principle is based on moderation. Many cadres were faced with the tension between family obligations and commitment to government policy; this could easily lead to accusations of corruption.

From 2011 to 2016, the growth rate of migrant workers has been declining, with growth rates of 3.4%, 3%, 1.7%, 1.3%, 0.4%, and 0.3%, respectively. The average age of migrant workers is now 39, and their average monthly income is 3275 RMB per month. The first generation of migrant workers were mainly unskilled manual workers, and after many years working in the cities, they are returning to their home villages (National Statistical Bureau 2018). With the money they have accumulated, skills they have learned, and knowledge of the city, they hope to find new opportunities in their home village. The Chinese government has recognized an impending decline in the number of semi-skilled workers in the cities. Consequently, by 2020, China is wanting to see an additional 100 million people granted urban *hukou,* which would grant them permanent residence in cities.

The One-Child Policy

Until the 1960s, the government had encouraged families to have as many children as possible because of Mao's belief that population growth empowered the country. The population grew from around 540 million in 1949 to 940 million in 1976. The one-child policy was introduced in 1979 and began to be formally phased out near the beginning of 2016 (Zhang 2017). According to the Chinese government, the policy prevented 400 million births although the claims have been questioned (Whyte et al. 2015).

Although the generation of Zhen and Cheng were free to give birth to as many children as they wished, the introduction of the one-child policy had immediate consequences for their children. In rural areas, the policy came into direct conflict with the labour demands of peasant households. The second generation struggled with the competing expectations to have children, especially a boy, to work with them and look after them in their old age, and their willingness to be loyal to government policy. Even though the one-child policy was applicable throughout China, local implementation of the policy often varied from district to district (Fong 2016). State employees could lose their jobs if they broke the regulation while people working in the countryside were less restrained by it. For example, Shun, Chun, and Dong were members of the CCP and were employed as teachers or officials; they especially found this challenging. This is sadly illustrated in the tension between Chun and his wife, Lan, regarding abortion. In contrast, a person like Xia, who was a businessman, paid the fine and had their second child added to their family documents.

The policy has given rise to extensive reflection on the social significance of the one-child family (Fong 2016). It can be seen that those born during the period of its implementation have few cousins, aunts, and uncles. They now face the problem of caring for both the husband's and the wife's ageing parents. The family often consists of two sets of grandparents, the working parents and one child who is studying. This is sometimes called the "4-2-1 Problem". China has experienced moderately low fertility for more than 30 years and now faces the challenge of a declining and yet ageing population (Zhang 2017). The personal care of the elderly is becoming an increasing problem for their children and grandchildren. This has resulted in some creative approaches such as two adjacent apartments being combined to provide extended accommodation suitable for grandparents, as well as parents and child. Many are now looking at the role of smart technology to assist with the care of the elderly.

The one-child policy resulted in some surprising outcomes for women. Whereas Zhen and her generation considered a woman's work was primarily to support the men in the family, the notion of gender equality and the one-child policy resulted in major changes. As Kai's story (Chap. 8) shows there was a growing sense of gender equality even when she was young, and the one-child policy has further encouraged this.

Zhen, like all women of her generation, wished that their first-born would be a boy, as this would not only enhance her status in the family but ensure the continuation of her husband's family line. When Zhen failed to produce a son, Cheng considered adoption as an option, but Zhen's persistence eventually resulted in the birth of a son. With the implementation of the one-child policy, parents continued to wish for a boy, and this, even though it was forbidden by the government, resulted in many female foetuses being aborted. The overall result is a shortage of young women of marriageable age. The gender imbalance enables young women to marry men of higher socioeconomic status while young men from poor farming areas are unable to find wives.

Nowadays, both daughters and sons are equally welcomed by parents. Educational attainment, career success, and family background are important spouse-selection criteria for men and women alike. Women who fall short of those standards can compensate with pleasant personalities, physical attractiveness, and the ability and willingness to do housework (Fong 2002). Future husbands are expected to provide the marital home, and this expectation remains an important determinant of whether a man can find a bride. This means a son and his parents need to inherit, buy, or rent housing by the time he is ready to marry. If a daughter and her parents can contribute to the marital home, this enhances the daughter's marriageability and comfort, rather than a requirement, as in the past (Fong and Kim 2011).

Parents are also now more willing to pay for their daughter's education so the female-to-male ratio of participation in higher education has increased from 0.35 in 1980 to 1.00 in 2010. Since 2010, more girls have been enrolled in tertiary education than boys. In 2013, female graduate students accounted for 49.0% of the total number of graduate students and 51.7% of undergraduate students are females. The better education of women results in better employment opportunities and social status. That means more women have career trajectories, which they don't want to jeopardize by marrying and having children while they are in their 20s and 30s. They are marrying later, or not at all.

Divorce is also becoming more common in China. Between 1979 and 2008, the divorce rate in China grew from 4% to 21.8%. According to figures released by the Ministry of Civil Affairs, the "crude divorce rate", which measures the number of separations for every 1000 people in the population, doubled in the decade 2006–2016, from 1.46 to 3.0. Even in the countryside, 70–80% of divorces are initiated by women. Viola Zhou, a Hong Kong-based sociologist, said that the soaring divorce rate could be partly attributed to changing attitudes among women, who have a greater sense of their own worth. "Women are now less willing to tolerate an unhappy marriage. They are more independent and financially equipped, and they can opt out if things go wrong" (Zhou 2017).

The second child policy was officially implemented in January 2016. In that year, there were 17.86 million births and a birth rate of 12.95%. In 2017, there were 17.23 million births and a birth rate of 12.43%. These figures are slightly up from an average of 16.44 million births for the period 2010–15. However, the proportion of births that were second children increased to 51% in 2017, an increase of 5% over the figure for 2016 (National Statistical Bureau 2018). The statistics from the National Statistical Bureau also shows that the main reasons why people do not plan to have a second child are the high cost of raising children, the shortage of child-care services, and the great pressure on women's career development. There is now speculation that the two-child policy may in 2019 (the year of the pig) be further relaxed to allow couples to have more children.

Education

In the past seven decades, educational policies in China have been characterized by bold moves that have resulted in new opportunities, especially for peasant families. Traditionally, rural children learned how to farm by working alongside their parents and older siblings. A father who had a specialist skill, such as Cheng—a vet—would want to see his eldest son learn those skills from him. If the parent did not have any such skills they could pay for their child to be taken on as an apprentice by those who did. This was how Cheng learned his skills as a vet, how Zhen learned to make shoes, and how Shi learned tailoring. Many practical life-skills however were learnt from the communal wisdom of the *jia*. Zhen learned much about buying and selling by going with her father to market and watching how he related with customers.

As Fei Xiaotong wrote in 1936, "Illiterate parents do not take school education very seriously" (Fei Xiaotong 1983: 33). This reflected the great inequalities in wealth and education between the cities and the countryside at the time. The PRC inherited a population that was 80% illiterate and a school system that provided enrolment to fewer than 40% and, in some areas, less than 20%. Even in 1982, the census indicated that 229 million people over the age of 15 were illiterate—about 35% of the adult population. According to the sixth national census of Statistics Bureau in 2010, the illiteracy rate was 4.08%, down 2.64% from that in 2000.

By 1951, some ten million rural peasants were studying at regular schools while many more attended *cunban* (village-run) schools and various adult education programmes. These *cunban* schools were locally managed and financed, and significantly expanded the basic-level educational opportunities available to rural children in the early years of the PRC. In 1951, one-third of all primary and general secondary school teachers were employed by *cunban* schools. In 1966, Mao Zedong proclaimed the start of a new educational era in which political recommendation and class background were the primary means of determining progress through the education system. "While educational quality certainly suffered greatly during the Cultural Revolution, the policies of this period appear to have been effective in promoting mass education among underserved groups including the rural population" (Hannum 1999: 199).

In Zhen's case, although she was brought up in a family in which only sons needed to have an elementary education, Zhen herself had a personal desire for education. She wanted all her children, both boys and girls, to go to school, but she also wanted them to acquire some practical skills. The poor status of the family was one of the reasons that Shun was given the opportunity by the commune cadres to train to be a primary school teacher. This was to prove to be a major benefit for all the younger children in the family. For the second generation, the ambition was to become an official or teacher with a permanent position.

In 1977, the *gaokao* examination resumed after the disruption of the Cultural Revolution. However, it was only in the early 1990s that students from the countryside effectively had an opportunity to pass the examination and go on to study at universities in the cities. Dong's story (Chap. 10) illustrates the shift that occurred at this time. Although he came top in his studies at 15, which enabled him to go on to vocational college, others in his cohort were later able to sit and to pass the *gaokao* and eventually gained jobs in the city. Meanwhile, Dong was working as a primary school teacher in the countryside. Nevertheless, through hard work, Dong was able to advance up the levels in the CCP.

Cheng and Zhen encouraged each of their children to work hard and to make education a priority. The various accounts of the children reading aloud every morning provide a vivid illustration. During the Maoist era, everyday life consisted of an endless cycle of work and "study sessions" aimed at developing socialist thinking. Working hard not only became a characteristic of Zhen's children but was also passed on to her grandchildren.

Today education has become a high priority for most families in China, and the government has sought to meet this demand through both state-run and private institutions. In 2016, the Chinese Ministry of Education reported that 37 million students were enrolled in 2852 higher-education institutions. This places China's gross enrolment rate into higher education for the cohort of 18–22-year-olds as 42.7%, and this is predicted to increase to 50% by 2020 (Ministry of Education 2017).

Modernization and Urbanization

As a nation, China has benefited greatly from globalization, especially after joining the WTO. The vast numbers of unskilled workers and a stable government meant that manufacturers in China were able to produce goods at a much lower cost than in developed countries. From 1980, modernization and urbanization became the keywords for development, as illustrated at the 2010 Shanghai World Exhibition with its slogan "Better City – Better Life". At that time, one could still see newly arrived migrant workers, with looks of astonishment, walking around the great shopping malls with their Louis Vuitton boutiques and Rolex showrooms. However, the numbers of new workers were already beginning to decline as the countryside slowly emptied of it multitudes.

For the millions of people like Qiu who went to the cities, life as a migrant labourer was at first strange and hard. They sought out people from their home areas to help them find a place to live and a job. Although the early years were a struggle, they knew that if they returned home, there would be few opportunities for them, apart from working in the fields. The great majority therefore stayed in the cities, became familiar with its ways, and often met partners with whom they established themselves in urban life. Many personal accounts have been recounted like those in Hsiao-Hung Pai's book *Scattered Sand* (Hsiao-Hung Pai 2012).

Although most migrants began as manual or factory workers, many began to set up a little business, such as selling fruit on the streets or running a noodle shop. If they had acquired some practical skills, they might make a living installing air-con units, painting apartments, or moving furniture. Through hard work and resilience, many flourished and managed to find a small niche in the burgeoning global market of which China was taking an ever-growing part. Nevertheless, this made some vulnerable to the changes in global trade. Qiu, for example, concentrated his business on the international market and was bankrupted by the global recession of 2008. His wife, in contrast, built her business on the domestic market, which was much less affected by the recession.

Urban migration had an immense impact on the countryside. The first wave of migrants were peasant farmers who could offer little more than their physical labour, and so took jobs building modern apartments for urban dwellers. The second wave has been a brain-drain of educated young people going to university or to work in the factories. Steadily, the population moved from the isolated communities leaving tens of thousands of villages with only old people and small children, until they were empty and abandoned—ghost villages. A common saying in China is: "When one lives in the village, one thinks of moving to the town; in the town, one thinks of moving to the provincial capital." Even with Zhen's family, one can see such a movement. Most of the second generation have moved from the village to the town, and the third has moved to the universities of the cities with a global perspective.

China's elderly population has grown substantially over the last 20 years. In 2000, China's population aged 65 and older was almost 90 million, and the elderly could number well over 300 million by 2050. In 2010, only 2% of the elderly were in institutions, and they were more likely to reside in urban areas. Like Zhen, most of China's elderly population have predominantly received care from their families. However, many of the elderly live either alone or with his or her spouse. The children have left home to work in the city and return home only for the spring holiday. These "empty nested elderly" amount to some 25%, but many, like Zhen's elderly friends, suffer loneliness (Wu et al. 2010).

There are an estimated 61 million children under the age of 18 who stayed at home under the care of either one of their parents or extended family members. These "left-behind children" only get together with their parents during the Chinese New Year. At ordinary times, they communicate with their parents through the mobile network. As Kai (Chap. 8) realizes, the repercussions of this separation can cause many social and psychological problems. One approach to this is the development of elementary boarding schools in rural areas, which accounts for 37.7% of the total number of rural children and 21.9% of all children.

The way of life in the countryside has changed with migration, and many local traditions and customs have almost become lost. Some have tried to capture the passing in life stories (Xinran 2008) or in photographs (Messmer and Hsin-mei 2013). The disappearance of the rich diversity and culture of the villages of China is regrettable, but recently, there have been major government efforts to retain the intangible heritage of the countryside through the encouragement of rural arts and crafts. Sichuan Province now organizes an Intangible Heritage Exhibition to revive these skills and to educate city dwellers about these traditions. This has been encouraged by the growth in the number of tourists from both home and abroad. The countryside has increasingly been marketed as an idyllic escape from the pollution and stress of city life. Around cities and towns, rural guesthouses have arisen to provide a cool haven to which families and friends can drive to enjoy each other's company whilst playing mahjong or cards. Agritourism, as it has come to be called, has proved a positive means of development in many rural areas.

The provision of electricity has been one of the most important driving forces of modernization in the countryside. At first, the supply was irregular and expensive so people could only afford a single light bulb in their home. Gradually, televisions became common as they were brought home as a gift by a son and daughter working in the city. By the beginning of the twenty-first century, electrification had spread through most of the countryside, and watching television has become a major preoccupation of both young and old. By 2010, Internet connectivity arrived, along with a mobile phone network. Although the digital divide still exists between city and countryside, the government continues to expand this new means of communication. Today, even small towns have Internet cafes, and WeChat has become widely popular throughout China, including the countryside.

As Hulme (2014) has pointed out, modern consumer society and consumerism as an ideology is now a global phenomenon and has developed rapidly in China. There are noted changes in the thinking and way of life of those still living in the countryside. Change has become an accepted norm of life, especially among the grandchildren studying at universities. Some changes are small and others are great. Zhen's family now prefer to gather together in a restaurant rather than cooking at home, partly because the family income is higher and partly because it has become part of their work lifestyle. Now there is little real preference as to whether the first baby is a boy or girl, and this is especially so since the lifting of the one-child policy.

In 2006, the central government drew up an important strategy called "Building a New Socialist Countryside" to coordinate urban and rural development and gear up national economic growth (Long et al. 2010). The measures included the improvement of traditional techniques of cultivation, and agricultural products and services were improved (Westmore 2015). In 2012, a government-sponsored survey identified 14 major areas of poverty in China. Two years later, the national targeted poverty alleviation programme was initiated, which aims to lift all people out of poverty and build "a moderately prosperous society by 2020". This book is about a family in one of these 14 poverty-stricken areas in China. The village of Jin'e and many of its neighbouring villages are rapidly changing as roads are being constructed to give vehicular access to every house, and material assistance is being given to the elderly and poor in the region.

* * *

The stories recounted here can be read in various ways. One is in how individualism has grown among the Chinese as they have been released first from the restraints of family and the Confucian social network, and later from the commune system imposed during the Mao era. Today, young people are exploring a new level of individual freedom never known before—freedom to travel, freedom to choose their own partner, freedom to indulge in leisure.

Kleinman has employed the term "quests for meaning" to discuss the wealth of research interviews he has undertaken among Chinese over many years (Kleinman 2011: 263–290). This is a useful way of discussing the narratives recounted here. It should be noted that Kleinman uses *quests* in the plural, as it is unrealistic to expect to identify a single quest in a society of over 1.3 billion people and even one individual having only one quest in their life. Nevertheless, for ordinary Chinese, there is a very practical perspective to the world and also to their quests.

The most common and ordinary quest is one that provides security for oneself and one's family. The quest for hundreds of millions of Chinese is to build and sustain a life that is relatively secure, filled with simple pleasures, and offers better chances for their children. For Zhen and Cheng, their hope was that through hard work and obedience to those in authority, they would have sufficient food and provision for the coming year. When opportunities did emerge, after initial hesitation, they were quick to respond in order to improve their lives. This is what Kleinman has called the "quest for happiness", which certainly is the foremost in the lives of Chinese people.

A second quest is what Yan has called the "drive for success" (Yunxiang Yan 2013). Whereas for Zhen, success was seen in terms of providing food for her family, for the second generation, success was in terms of leaving the land, obtaining a good job, and making money, while for the third generation, success is seen in terms of academic achievement. For the third generation, the ambition has grown from passing the *gaokao* to become one of seeking the best education available worldwide. However, as Yan comments, this can lead to the need to make choices between competing issues. "The drive for success, while challenging both traditional Confucian ethics and Communist ethics, also creates moral predicaments for the individual, forcing her to choose between competing values, to judge right and wrong and good and bad and to take action accordingly" (Yunxiang Yan 2013: 273). The choice between loyalty to the family or to the directives of the Party can be one such struggle.

A third quest Kleinman has described is an important quest by women for a valued status. This is clearly seen in the fourth daughter's story, where as a child, she was sent to bed first to warm the bed for her two younger brothers with whom she shared a bed. Mao said, "Women hold up half the sky," but women continue to struggle to achieve a valid status and identity. The greater number of women to men in higher education reveals something of their ongoing quest, as does the increasing number of divorces initiated by women.

Fourth, not all quests relate to personal success or status. In 2008, one of the authors was teaching in Sichuan during the massive earthquake and as was impressed by the sudden rise in volunteers coming from across China. Many came from wealthy homes in Beijing, Tianjin, and Shanghai. Although one reason for this could be the socialist emphasis for Party members to "serve the people", amongst most of the volunteers, there was a genuine humanitarian concern in response to such a disaster. Amongst students, there is a new environmental consciousness and an interest in human rights and consumer protection. The stories recorded here also show a genuine concern for the improvement in the countryside and assistance to those who are struggling.

Bibliography

Chang, L.T. 2010. *Factory Girls*. London: Picador.
Cleverley, John. 1991. *The Schooling of China: Tradition and Modernity in Chinese Education*. Sydney: Allen & Unwin.
Ebrey, Patricia Buckley. 1991. *Confucianism and Family Rituals in Imperial China: A Social History of Writing about Rites*. Princeton: Princeton University Press.
Fei Xiaotong. 1939. *Peasant Life in China*. London: Routledge & Kegan Paul.
———. 1983. *Chinese Village Close-Up*. Beijing: New World Press.
Fong, Mei. 2016. *One Child: The Story of China's Most Radical Experiment*. London: One World Publications.
Fong, Vanessa L. 2002. "China's One-Child Policy and the Empowerment of Urban Daughters." *American Anthropologist* 104 (4): 1098–1109.
Fong, Vanessa L., and Sung won Kim. 2011. "Anthropological Perspectives on Chinese Children, Youth, and Education." In *A Companion to the Anthropology of Education*, edited by Bradley A.U. Levinson and M Pollock, 333-. London: Blackwell.
Hannum, Emily. 1999. "Political Change and the Urban-Rural Gap in Basic Education in China, 1949–1990." *Comparative Education Review* 43 (2): 193–211.
Hsiao-Hung Pai. 2012. *Scattered Sand: The Story of China's Rural Migrants*. London: Verso Books.
Hulme, A. 2014. *The Changing Landscape of China's Consumerism*. Oxford: Elsevier.
Jacka, Tamara. 2006. *Rural Women in Urban China: Gender, Migration and Social Change*. New York: M.E.Sharpe.
Jankowia, W.R., and Robert L. Moore. 2016. *Family Life in China*. Cambridge: Polity Press.
Kleinman, Arthur. 2011. *Deep China: The Moral Life of the Person: What Anthropology and Psychiatry Tell Us about China Today*. University of California Press.
Lee, Sing. 2011. "Depression: Coming of Age in China." In *Deep China*, edited by Arthur Kleinman, 177–212. Berkeley: University of California Press.
Li, Cheng. 2010. *China's Emerging Middle Class: Beyond Economic Transformation*. Washington: Brookings Ins. Press.
Long, Hualou, Yansui Liu, Xiubin Li, and Yufu Chen. 2010. "Building New Countryside in China: A Geographical Perspective." *Land Use Policy* 27 (2): 457–70.
Messmer, M., and Chuang Hsin-mei. 2013. *China's Vanishing Worlds: Countryside, Traditions, and Cultural Spaces*. MIT Press.

Ministry of Education. 2017. "Report on Quality of Higher Education in China." Beijing.
National Statistical Bureau. 2018. "The 'two-Child Policy' Continues to Show Positive Results in 2017." Beijing.
Ruf, Gregory A. 1998. *Cadres and Kin: Making a Socialist Village in West China, 1921–1991.* Stanford University Press.
Thompson, W. 2010. "China's Rapidly Aging Population." *Today's Research on Aging* 20: 1–5.
Westmore, Ben. 2015. "'Agricultural Reforms and Bridging the Gap for Rural China', OECD Economics Department Working Papers, No. 1218." Paris. OECD.
Whyte, Martin King, Wang Feng, and Yong Cai. 2015. "Challenging Myths about China's One-Child Policy." *China Journal* 74 (74): 144–59.
Wu, Zhen Qiang, Liang Sun, Ye Huan Sun, Xiu Jun Zhang, Fang Biao Tao, and Guang Hui Cui. 2010. "Correlation between Loneliness and Social Relationship among Empty Nest Elderly in Anhui Rural Area, China." *Aging and Mental Health* 14 (1): 108–12.
Xinran. 2008. *China Witness.* London: Vintage.
Yan, Y. 2010. "The Chinese Path to Individualization." *The British Journal of Sociology* 61 (3): 489–512.
———. 2011. "The Individualization of the Family in Rural China." *Boundary 2* 38 (1). Duke University Press: 203–29.
Yan, Yunxiang. 2002. "Courtship, Love and Premarital Sex in a North China Village." *China Journal* 48: 28–53.
———. 2013. "The Drive for Success and the Ethics of the Striving Individual." In *Ordinary Ethics in China*, edited by Charles Stafford, 263–91. London: Bloomsbury.
Zhang, J. 2017. "The Evolution of China's One-Child Policy and Its Effects on Family Outcomes." *Journal of Economic Perspectives* 31 (1): 141–60.
Zhang, Li. 2001. *Strangers in the City.* Stanford: Stanford University Press.
Zhou, Viola. 2017. "Marriage Rate down, Divorce Rate up as More Chinese Couples Say "I Don't" or "I Won't Any More"." *South China Morning Post*, September 6.

Glossary

Chunjie	春节	Spring Festival
Cun	村	Village
Cunban	村办	Village-run; often used for a village-run school
Dachuanlian	大串联	A revolutionary tour around the country by Red Guards
Dai hua	带花	A stage in a traditional marriage
Daling nuqingnian	大龄女青年	Leftover lady
Die	爹	Colloquial for father; daddy
Fenjia	分家	Traditional practice of dividing the family
Ganbu	干部	A government cadre
Gaokao	高考	National University Entrance Examination
Gongliang	公粮	Harvest tax on peasants, now abolished
Gongxifacai	恭喜发财	Greeting "May you be happy and prosperous"
Guangboticao	广播体操	Gymnastics broadcast
Guanxi	关系	Social relationships
Hong Weibin	红卫兵	Red Guards
Hukou	户口	Household registration
Jia	家	Family
Jiejie	姐姐	Older sister
Jinfanwan	金饭碗	Literally "iron rice bowl"—secure and well-paid job
Kaigeng	开庚	Stage in a traditional marriage
Kanrenhu	看人户	A stage in a traditional marriage
MaozhuxiYulu	毛主席语录	Quotations from Chairman Mao
Meimei	妹妹	Younger sister
Mu	亩	Unit of land measurement, 0.165 acre or 666.5 square metres
Nainai	奶奶	Grandma
Popo	婆婆	Dialect "Grandmother"

Shousui	守岁	To stay up late on New Year's Eve
Songbang	松绑	Literally "to untie", relax restrictions
Suanming	算命	Fortune-teller
Wu Xing	五行	Five elements (metal, wood, water, fire, and earth)
Xian	县	A county
Xiangzhen	乡镇	A township
Xiaonian	小年	Small celebration for New Year
Yuanxiao	元宵	Last day of the Spring Festival, also called Lantern Festival
Zhanzhu zheng	暂住证	Temporary residence card
Zhengyue	正月	First month of the lunar year
Zhi qing	知青	Educated youth (sent to work in the countryside during the Cultural Revolution)
Zhuifengzi	捉疯子	Literally "chasing madman"—a children's game
Zou dong xi	走东西	Literally "walking gift"—one stage in a traditional marriage
Zuoyuezi	坐月子	Literally "sitting the month"—a new mother was required to stay home for a month after childbirth

GPSR Compliance

The European Union's (EU) General Product Safety Regulation (GPSR) is a set of rules that requires consumer products to be safe and our obligations to ensure this.

If you have any concerns about our products, you can contact us on

ProductSafety@springernature.com

In case Publisher is established outside the EU, the EU authorized representative is:

Springer Nature Customer Service Center GmbH
Europaplatz 3
69115 Heidelberg, Germany

www.ingramcontent.com/pod-product-compliance
Lightning Source LLC
LaVergne TN
LVHW011006250326
834688LV00004B/103